My Journey From Aircraft A&P to CEO

Robert R. Cupery

Aircraft Window Repairs

ISBN: 979-8-9892415-0-7 (Softcover)
ISBN: 979-8-9892415-1-4 (Hardcover)
ISBN: 979-8-9892415-2-1 (Ebook)

Published by:

Cupery Corporation, d/b/a Aircraft Window Repairs
2207 Border Ave.
Torrance, CA 90501

(310) 212-7173
www.aircraftwindowrepairs.com

Endorsements

"For as long as I have known Bob Cupery, he has always expressed the desire to have his own business and make a creditable contribution to his chosen field of aircraft maintenance. Exposure to in-flight equipment failures, while employed as a flight engineer, created the perfect entrée for Bob to pursue his sought-after business venture."

– Don Short, former Air Force One pilot and former director of flight operations/chief pilot, Northrop Corporation and MCA, Inc.

High praise for Bob Cupery:

"Success in your business does not surprise me after all the excellent maintenance service you provided on the Northrop G-II during our travels throughout the world in support of the F-5 aircraft."

– Thomas V. Jones, past president/CEO, Northrop Corporation.

Contents

Foreword

The Gulfstream II flight crew, from left, Pilot Don Short,
Flight Engineer Bob Cupery, and Co-Pilot Ed Hahn

Bob Cupery and I have a long history, both personally and professionally.
Some of my first impressions of him occurred when Bob served as
an aircraft mechanic/flight engineer/steward while crewing our new
executive jet. He was a dedicated professional with a goal, yet it remained
unrealized for many years.

That goal was to have his own company bearing his name. Barely out of airframe and powerplant (A&P) school, Bob was already an enthusiastic young man with high personal and professional standards. He possessed, to an unusual degree, unlimited growth potential.

Some of Bob's work experiences, although horrendous, unimaginable, and not caused by his hand, served to guide him like a shiny object on the distant horizon toward his eventual goal of owning his personal business.

Windshields on the jet we flew experienced an alarming failure rate. It was something the plane's manufacturer was keenly aware of, but unable to quickly resolve. Bob worried about this dilemma as he worked to replace the jet's windows in some of those cursed situations to which he was exposed. He came to realize there could be a profitable future in aircraft windows, if they were properly maintained or repaired. He knew he could save plane operators a lot of money instead of requiring them to buy pricey replacements.

Earlier in Bob's career as a flying crewman, his leadership qualities were recognized when he was honored as Airman of the Month for his U.S. Air Force flying unit. He mentored entry-level mechanics under his supervision by offering encouragement and techniques that would ensure their success.

That leadership trait, along with his warm, friendly interaction, created a subtle transfer of confidence he extended on a personal level to his passengers, which earned Bob many accolades and letters of appreciation. From captains of industry to popular celebrities, as well as our own Northrop executives, Bob served through purveying our corporate hospitality.

A few years later, with a sound business plan in place, Bob set about organizing his own company. Choosing a niche to offer specialized aircraft products and services to an impressive list of clients, Aircraft Window Repairs became Bob's focus as he led his company forward for more than four decades. By any measure, his company offers a quality service without peer and a reputation built on safety, as well as operational excellence. When creativity meets ambition, a wonderful thing can happen. Bob Cupery proved that on the job and in his business.

Don Short
Major, USAF, Retired
Presidential pilot to former President Lyndon Johnson
Andrews AFB, Maryland

Director and Chief Pilot
Corporate Air Transportation
Northrop Corporation
Los Angeles, California

Chief Pilot of the Aviation Staff and Vice President
MCA Service Corporation
Universal City, Calif.

Acknowledgements

First and foremost, I want to thank my loving and beautiful wife, Kathi, for her countless hours of support. She has listened to my countless flight stories and encouraged me to share them with others.

Finally, a big shout out and thank you to Editor Greg Gerber for his professionalism in writing, editing and organizing this book.

As a trustee at the Western Museum of Flight at Zamperini Field in Torrance, Calif., I would like to acknowledge my fellow trustees and volunteers for their tireless effort in preserving the history of aviation and their contributions to the women in aerospace.

Robert R. Cupery
November 2023

Chapter 1

Early life

Cupery family, circa 1955, from left: Bob, Larry, Ruby, Laverne, Rink, Eli, and Stan.

I was born in Beaver Dam, Wis., in 1944 to Rink Eli Cupery and Ruby Elizabeth Hiama. We were basically two families. My brother, Larry, was fourteen years older than me; my sister, Laverne, was twelve years older; and my brother, Stan, was three years older.

My father was a bank president for thirty years. As a result, we knew everyone in the small town of Friesland, Wis., with a population of about 300, including pets. Located about twenty miles northwest of Beaver Dam, the village was about one-mile square and included a school, hardware store, my dad's bank, a plastics factory, gas station, a few repair stations, and not much else.

In 1950, Laverne, Stan and I joined our parents in moving to Bellflower, Calif., which is a suburb of Los Angeles about six miles north of Long Beach Airport. By then, Larry had joined the U.S. Air Force.

While on that trip in my dad's new 1950 Plymouth, we were passing an oil tanker truck when a hose came loose and dumped oil all over the car from top to bottom. We watched as some men tried washing the car completely with gasoline, which turned the car from a nice shiny vehicle into a very faded green. It could have been worse if the gasoline had somehow caught on fire. I don't remember much about that experience, other than my dad's anger, which the long, hot trip made even worse because the car didn't have air conditioning and the interior reeked of petroleum.

Once settled into our new home, we enrolled in Bellflower Christian School. My first teacher was Mrs. Green. I don't remember her first name, but we didn't get off to a particularly satisfying start. I remember her bringing me home in tears one day because she could not control me. I don't remember if I was assigned another teacher or if I transferred to another school. All I remember is that I did not see Mrs. Green again.

The only other things I remember about growing up in California was that the area in which we lived was referred to as the "dairy valley." There were about 400 dairies in the area milking more than 100,000 cows in what is now the city of Cerritos. Our family raised chickens in the backyard, and the mooing of cows could be frequently heard, especially early in the morning.

One day, I almost got hit by a car while walking home from school. Although I was not hurt, the woman who was driving was pretty shaken up. Another time I was running away from some bullies when I tried to hide in a cement drainage pipe, and bumped my head on the pipe. Fortunately, they couldn't find me and I managed to escape, but I did need some stitches on my forehead. That was around Christmas time, and I still have pictures of me with my head in bandages while playing with my new electric train.

Mom missed Wisconsin

Our time in California was short because my mother thought the Los Angeles area was too busy and she missed her parents. That was okay with me because I adored my Grandpa Carl, who always took time to talk to me. On the other hand, my grandmother, Mae, was really mean. She kept pinching or pulling my ears. I don't remember why, but I suspect I deserved it.

Upon our return, my dad had started a new profession selling cars in nearby Randolph, Wis., for a Ford dealership. It was owned by Olie Bosine and his cousin. His other cousin, Clyde Newmandor, lived in Waupun and owned a Pontiac dealership.

I attended Friesland Grade School where there were twenty-four students in my first-grade class. I was a pretty good student at the time and received many gold stars for reading. The bad part is that I also got into a lot of fights with other kids. I remember playing baseball one day when an argument broke out regarding whose turn it was to bat next. A scuffle ensued and I wound up hitting my friend, Rodney Kok, with a bat. He had a gash to his eyebrow, so I went into the school and told my teacher that someone had hit Rodney with a bat. When my teacher asked me who hit him, I sheepishly admitted that I was the one with a bat.

Sometimes, I would return home with torn shirts or even broken eye glasses. My parents had received several bad reports from school, and they were convinced I was a real troublemaker. But, during a parent-teacher meeting in 1958, my teacher, Eldon Gaffenty, who was also the principal, told my parents he was convinced I would definitely do well in life. That made my parents feel much better about my future prospects.

That summer, my dad wanted to try his hand at farming, so we moved to the Jones Farm, which was about 160 acres in size with part of the Fox River running through the property. It was beautiful, but there was no running water on the farm, nor was there an inside toilet. That made Wisconsin winters particularly challenging while traipsing through snow to use the outhouse. However, my uncle, Nick Cupery, who owned the hardware store in Friesland, graciously installed running water and an indoor toilet, which made life much more enjoyable for all of us.

During canning season, which spanned about three months, my father would manage the day-to-day work on the farm while my mother operated a food stand in the canning factory to feed employees at all hours of the day. Even my father would help out at night. I would be very busy during that time using my bike to deliver supplies to the food stand, like ice blocks, hamburgers, hotdogs, etc.

A buddy, Pete Deboer, and I would stand on the roof of a small building in the driveway and steal peas from the vine after they ripened, but before they made their way to a canning facility. Pete and I would often bike more than ten miles just to see each other.

The canning factory used migrant workers to help harvest produce, and they would live in bunk houses by the plant. I would walk around that neighborhood collecting empty pop bottles, which I could take back to the store and collect a nickel for each bottle. It was good money for a twelve-year-old.

When I visited the bunk houses, I got to know some of the workers, and they would often strike up a conversation with me. A few of the men let me "review" their girly magazines, which provided even more motivation to visit.

Off the farm

My father attempted to buy the Jones farm, which included a four-story house. Unfortunately, the sale didn't go through, and we had to move again.

By then, my sister, Laverne, married George Levey. He helped us move back to the Four Corners area just outside of Randolph, Wis. This time, my father was successful in buying the Jones farm, so we moved back. My brother, Larry, also got engaged and my parents drove to New York to meet his fiancé, Joyce, when she arrived from England. It was a very busy time with two of my siblings getting married in the same year.

Once Larry and Joyce were married, they moved in with us and took over the second floor, which also had a full kitchen. My father helped Larry get started in farming, and my job was to feed the chickens and mow the very large lawn by using a push reel mower. I also had to feed the yearlings, which were young cows. I would drive the faded 1950 Plymouth to the very back of the cornfield, mowing down corn along the way. I would cut the short corn in two rows and fill the car's trunk with the harvested corn. The early harvest was done that way so when the rest of the corn was harvested, the tractor would have a path to follow. The corn in the trunk would be used to feed the yearlings.

One day I wanted to see how fast I could drive through the hayfield on my way back to the barn. So, with my eyes staring at the speedometer, I pushed the gas pedal as far as it would go. When I finally looked up, I was at the end of the field and about to drive onto the dirt road, which had large trees on the edge. I turned the steering wheel sharply, which caused the car to spin out and scatter the corn in the trunk all over the field. I'm fortunate that I didn't roll the car. There was grass embedded in the rims of the tires, which I had to remove before my father discovered it.

But, I didn't learn my lesson about driving safely. Another day, while going to get the corn, I was playing a game with my dog, Sporty. I would step on the gas, and he'd run over to the other side. When I let off the gas, he would cross again. We had a fun rhythm going until I faked him out and accidentally ran over him. He died in my arms.

In 1955, my dad stopped selling cars and decided to buy a meat-cutting plant and storage lockers in Friesland. The Cupery & De Young Storage facility, which was next door to the meat-cutting plant, was still in operation in 2022.

My father would cut the meat, then package and store it in the lockers. My job was to trim fat off the pork, grind hamburger and tend to the counter when customers came in. I remember cutting my hand on the food slicer while slicing meat for a customer who was complaining about how long it took to prepare his order. I bled on his meat, but wrapped it up for him.

Around that time, my mother started a restaurant next door, and I would help there occasionally as well. I was eleven years old and my father was the town's mayor at the time.

My friend, Larry Dykstra, worked for Cliff's Electric. That business shared the same telephone party line as our firm. Back then, telephones were really expensive, so people often shared a line. All calls were processed by an operator. To get her attention, we would have to crank the phone, which rang at the switchboard. It was possible for people to listen in to other conversations all the time. It also meant that Larry and I could talk to each other by simply picking up the phone at the same time. It was a fun thing to do during our spare time.

Larry and I would often get into mischief while working at Cliff's Electric. I remember putting a metal plate on a chair people would sit on so they could watch cartoons on the display television. Then, we hooked it up to an electric fence and shocked them just for fun. One guy got so mad that he broke the chair.

Whenever I seemed to get in trouble, my brother-in-law, George Levey, always came to my defense. When my parents would tell others about all the bad things I had done the previous week, George would always say, "Not our Bob." When people were talking about someone driving through town at a hundred miles per hour, George would say, "Not our Bob." Of course, it was really me having a lot of fun getting into mischief.

We grew up in a Christian home and my father served as a deacon and elder at our local church. We went to church every Sunday morning, followed by Sunday School and another service on Sunday night. I also attended a catechism class on Monday nights. So, my misbehavior reflected poorly upon my parents and how they raised me.

My first car

In 1960, I bought my first car when I was just fifteen years old. It had belonged to my father's cousin, Clyde, who owned a Pontiac dealership in Waupun, Wis., about fifteen miles from my home. It happened to be the first car Clyde sold in 1937, so the vehicle was rather old. It had been damaged when a sheet of ice slid down the dealership's tin roof and caved in the car's top. I bought it for just forty dollars, but it was like new with only 17,000 miles on it.

On the way home, I pushed the car to one hundred miles per hour. But, I didn't realize my father was following me. I was severely scolded when we arrived home, but I didn't get into any serious trouble.

The first thing I did to the car was to grab a hacksaw and cut the top off. Then I removed the fenders and took it to a welding shop next to the mill. Pete, the owner, welded on motorcycle fenders. I painted the engine chrome and soon had what looked like a California hot rod.

George hired me to work in his feed mill to grind corn into feed for cows and then deliver it to local farmers. It was not unusual for me to shovel sixteen tons of corn daily, six days a week. For comparison's sake, a bushel weighed fifty-six pounds, which meant I was shoveling more than 570 bushels of corn every day. During the rare slack times in processing corn, I also had to unload train cars full of different minerals.

Teflon tape

Although it was a very busy time at the mill, I was also tasked with rolling Teflon tape onto smaller rolls for my father, who was now president and owner of Friesland Plastics Company. My uncle, Martin Cupery, had learned about Teflon when he worked for Dupont, and brought some samples home to show my father. Dad loved the product and started another company with Martin that became one of the first plants in the world to manufacture Teflon tape and ship it to all fifty states. The tape was used to seal pipes.

As the company's assistant marketing representative, I remember attending trade shows in Milwaukee and Chicago where people stood three- to four-deep to learn more about Teflon tape. It was so successful that my father sold his meat-cutting business a short time later.

I parked my 1937 Pontiac in one of the factory's empty warehouses to change the electrical wiring. One day, an employee was burning grass when the fire got away from him and ignited the warehouse. Fire departments from three nearby towns were called in to fight the blaze. The firefighters knocked a hole in the warehouse wall, sprayed my car with water, and allowed me to drive it out with my brand-new toolbox in the trunk. The tires were scorched, and the paint blistered, but I drove it out. I still have that toolbox today, and it has traveled throughout the world with me.

Around this time, my best buddy, Pete, and I visited a farmer who had a Model A Ford in his chicken coop. We thought we could get the vehicle running, so he bought it for forty dollars. We purchased another battery, some gas, and a tire pump. After getting the car running, we drove it to his father's farm. My friend rebuilt everything and cleaned all the chicken poop out of it. So, now we each had a car to drive around during winter and summer. Neither of us had a license, so we did a lot of off-road driving. I remember both of us driving our cars in parades during high school homecoming days.

Pete still has the Model A, which we drive whenever I visit Wisconsin. I sold my Pontiac, but I don't remember what price I received. I'm sure it was more than my initial forty-dollar investment.

In high school, I remember taking English class with Ms. Tropper. Her rule was that if a student ever came to class without a pen, he or she would receive a zero and F or the day. One day that happened to me. I asked a classmate, Terry Moldenhaur, to loan me a pen because he had a pocket full of them. However, he wouldn't lend me one, even when I told him that he'd be sorry. My threats didn't work, and I got my F for the day. After class, I followed Terry into the restroom and, a few minutes later, you could follow a trail of his blood to the principal's office. He eventually went to the doctor. As one might expect, I had to speak with the principal, and he told me I was acting like an animal. I would pay for my impulsiveness a few weeks later.

When the F showed up on my report card for English, I had to show it to the football coach. He knew the rules wouldn't allow me to play in the homecoming football game that night. So, he took it down to Ms. Tropper's room. When he returned, the F had been changed to a D- so that I could play in the game. Needless to say, I didn't much care for Ms. Tropper or Terry.

A knack for knocking heads

When 1959 rolled around, it was a really exciting time in my life. I had discovered girls and football, both of which I truly love.

My brother, Stan, was already a star on the football team and was frequently mentioned in the local paper. Stan and another player, John Tamminga, were referred to as the "Touchdown Twins" because they could catch anything thrown in their direction. For many years after they graduated, their coach, Mr. Treawon, still attended their class reunions.

Coach Treawon inquired about me and wondered if I would be trying out for football as a freshman. Shoveling sixteen tons of corn a day paid off well, as did unloading boxcars full of corn from 7 a.m. to 7 p.m. some days. I had plenty of strength in my arms to move people around. When I joined the team, I was given a leather helmet with screws holding the facemask on. As luck had it, the senior tackle wasn't doing his job and, because I could perform better, I got the chance to manhandle opposing players on offense and defense.

Not only did I earn a letter for my effort, but I was awarded an unbreakable plastic Rawling helmet. But, I hit opposing players so hard that I cracked three helmets in three years.

Football became my favorite sport because it allowed me to utilize my mind and all my muscles. The coach kept track of our performance and awarded apples to players when the season ended. We were given one apple for tackling opposing players for a loss, and two apples for sacking the quarterback. The apples were presented at the end-of-season banquet. One year, I received two grocery bags full of apples!

By the time I was a junior at Cambria High School, my time was pretty well occupied with either football, basketball, baseball, or track, depending upon the season. But, I still found time for girls.

Three nights a week, I worked at Friesland Plastic Company. The plant switched from manufacturing rolls of tape to producing Teflon strips. Since it was a new company, budgets were low, and no unnecessary help was employed full-time. Because I had previous training in auto mechanics, I was assigned to maintain the company's vehicles at night.

My love for music

During the summer, I played tuba for a circus band. The pay was low, but I did enjoy playing alongside older musicians. At a competition in Verona, Wis., I played a trumpet solo on my tuba, which resulted in a first-place tie. That experience helped me qualify for a state music competition where my tuba solo earned an A on my evaluation.

After that achievement, I received a letter from professors Emmett Sarig and Edward Hugdahl, chairmen of the music program at the University of Wisconsin Extension. They asked me to play in the state 4-H band at the university as well as at the Wisconsin State Fair. With my skill, I tied for the first chair position in that band.

This was really an exciting moment because guys and gals from all over the United States enjoyed an opportunity to perform at the Conrad Hilton Hotel in Chicago. After practicing for weeks, we headed off to Chicago. The experience of being away from home—really away from home—helped encourage me to venture out on my own later in life.

I had previously traveled to large cities with my father to attend business conferences, industrial expositions, and to visit customers. But, the trip to Chicago was special because it was based on my own achievement. Phonograph records were made of our performance and, based on sales, people must have thought we were very good.

Exploring aviation

It was around this point in my life that I developed an interest in aircraft. During summer vacation, the band director in a nearby town asked me if I would also play in his high school band. He was a pilot, so I offered to march in his band if he would trade my time for flying lessons in his Porterfield CP65 Collegiate two-seat, single-engine aircraft.

The deal was made, and I had my first flight. We flew off that grass strip many times before I was forced to give up flying lessons after my mother had learned of our deal. Apparently, she desired to have her son around a while longer. Out of respect to her, and to keep peace in the family, I gave up flying. However, I caught the bug and just knew I wanted a career in aviation.

Ironically, I was reunited with that CP65 aircraft at a high school reunion in the 1980s. It so happened that the auto dealer in Cambria had acquired the plane. But, when he got divorced, the court awarded everything to his wife. Enraged over the decision, he killed her, and all the property wound up in an auction where one of my former classmates bought the plane. It was thrilling to be able to sit in it once again.

During my final year of high school, I became more involved in sports as the captain of our football team. The extra-curricular activities added more stress to the usual academic load. Yet, I managed to graduate on June 1, 1962. It still seems like yesterday when I reflect back on those four years.

I was up to my neck in work the summer after graduation. I landed a job in a feed mill as a recordkeeper in the evenings, and I used my muscles to move feed sacks during the day. When I arrived at the mill each morning, I was given a stack of work orders showing how much feed needed to be distributed to local farms. This involved taking an empty truck to a farm, shoveling it full of corn and driving the load back to the mill where it was ground, bagged, and delivered back to the farm, where the bags were neatly stacked in a barn. I moved an average of seventeen tons of corn every day. If there was ever a slack period at the mill, I was tasked with unloading trainloads of various minerals parked nearby.

I attended two more industrial fairs as an assistant marketing representative for the plastic factory that summer. These trips, one in Chicago and the other in Milwaukee, were learning opportunities for me because they exposed me to a whole new way of life. Attending the conventions would help me in my own business several years later.

The floors at the convention centers were crowded as businessmen walked through the various displays. My job was to staff our booth for short intervals and explain the features and benefits of our new Teflon product.

The exposure to the sales life was useful and very interesting. It prompted me to enter a career in sales to market my aircraft window repair business many years later.

However, I desired even more freedom and, in my mind, the only way to do that was to volunteer for military service.

Chapter 2

Childhood photos

Me, at age 4, with a cat on the family farm.

As a youngster, my job was to feed the yearling calves.

My brother, Stan, and I shortly before my second birthday.

Me around my sixth birthday.

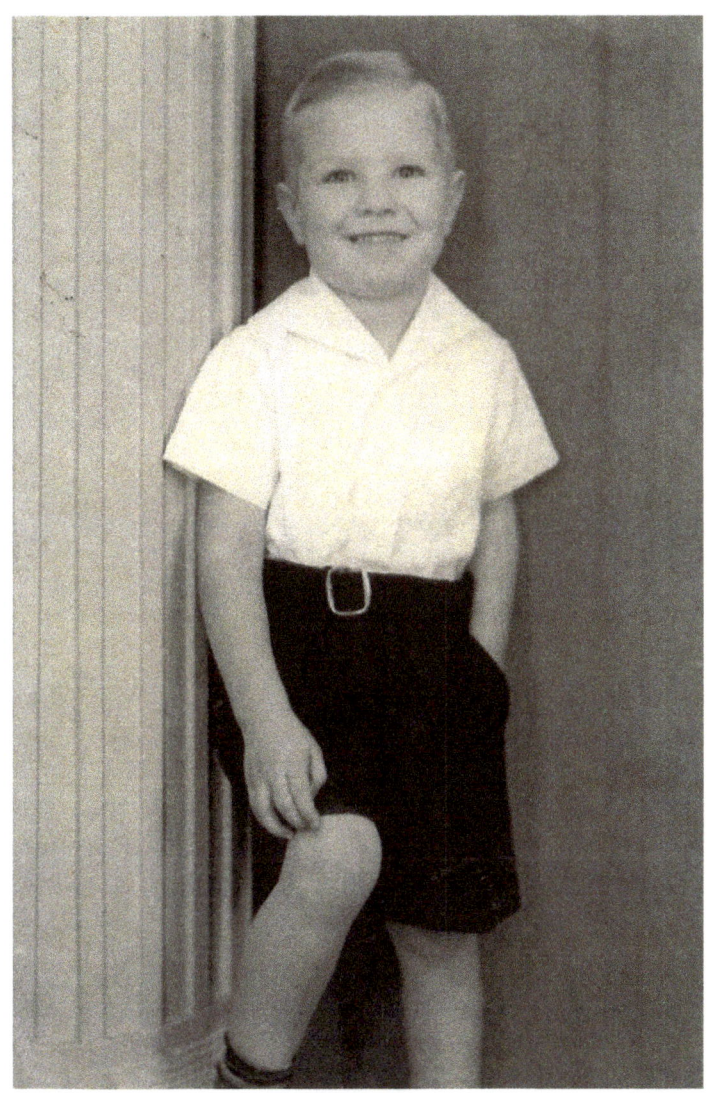

Me around age 3.

Me playing with a train set I received for Christmas in 1951.

By 1953, I was tending to the chickens which roamed on the farm.

Me with a pheasant I shot in 1958.

Stan and I playing football.

Me in my Boy Scout uniform in 1956

Chapter 3

Introduction to aviation

My high school senior portrait taken in 1962.

During my senior year of football, I experienced what you might call a divine intervention. On a kickoff play, I was on the receiving end of a cross-body block just below my right knee. My body was pushed over, but my knee stayed straight, resulting in a dislocation.

Dreaming of seeing the world, I planned on joining the U.S. Marine Corps after graduation. But, because of my knee, I was told I wouldn't qualify. However, I learned the U.S. Air Force would let me join. It turned out to be very good luck for me. Enlisting was really quite easy. In fact, it went so fast that I can't remember all the details. The recruiter gave me a bus ticket to Milwaukee where I was put on a plane to San Antonio, Texas, and dressed in an ugly, oversized green suit before I had time to reconsider my decision.

Basic training started out pretty tough and I quickly learned that marching ten hours a day wasn't for me. So, instead of wasting all my free time on Sunday, I started asking questions and reading bulletin boards in church.

A few days after basic training began, the Air Force discovered I knew how to play a musical instrument, so I was transferred to a drum and bugle squadron. It was still basic training, but I enjoyed it much more even though it added another two months to my basic training assignment.

The music practice sessions replaced about three hours of marching, and I enjoyed local trips to perform for people on base and in the community. We also got to practice in an air-conditioned building while the other men were stuck marching in the heat. Being in the band also earned me my first stripe as I headed off to advanced technical training.

Through this experience, I learned to ignore what most people told me would be impossible. They said I would never be allowed to serve in the military, but I volunteered and it was a life-changing decision. Had I not joined the military; I would likely have remained in Friesland shoveling corn or snow for many years.

Off to jet maintenance school

Once I completed basic training, I found myself in Amarillo, Texas, going to jet aircraft maintenance school to learn how to work on F-100 fighter jets.

I enjoyed each class and could follow the curriculum quite easily, thanks to my prior experience in completing automotive repairs for the plastics company. My father also gave me $500 to enroll in a night school sponsored by General Motors on Monday nights. The benefit of attending that course was that I got to miss a Bible study at church. Yet, once I started studying the mechanics of aircraft operation, I was hooked. A new passion and career was opened to me.

When I completed maintenance training, I originally hoped to be assigned to a permanent duty station in Florida or some exotic location in Europe. However, the Air Force must have sensed that I liked cold weather because I was ordered to report to Wurtsmith Air Force Base near Oscoda, Mich. That is where I served with the 445th Fighter Interceptor Squadron. It was an important assignment because the base housed the nuclear-armed B-52 Stratofortress bombers during the Cold War.

The fighter jets patrolled the North American Distant Early Warning (DEW) line along the Canadian border during the Vietnam War. It was a relatively bland experience since the base only went on alert twice, once when the Soviet Union placed missiles in Cuba, and again when President Kennedy was assassinated.

Oscoda was not as bad as I thought it would be when I first learned of the assignment. Yes, the winters were cold, but the hunting, fishing, skiing, and natural scenic beauty of lower Michigan and Lake Huron made up for the freezing temperatures.

The first eight months I was stationed there, I completed an on-the-job (OJT) training program to learn about the aircraft I would maintain. The reward for passing one test and moving on to the next higher skill level was that I earned another stripe. As a senior airman, I could train two lower-ranked airmen who were completing their own OJT. One of these men arrived at Wurtsmith the same time I did. My training was so successful that he went on to serve as a crew chief on two F-101 aircraft, one of which was the base commander's jet. That's a prestigious job and the fact that I prepared him to work on the colonel's aircraft reflected well on my ability, too.

Later, I worked on what was called a periodic inspection dock where aircraft were evaluated at various stages of their operational lives. However, the unit always seemed to be behind the ball in completing inspections on time. That threatened to reduce operational readiness of the entire squadron.

My first management job

I suspected the problem rested with management working on night shifts, so I volunteered to work that slot. As a result, I received exactly what I wanted, which was a free hand in supervising all the maintenance technicians working the night shift.

This consisted of planning, organizing and supervising seventeen men, and coordaining their work with five separate repair shops. I took the opportunity very seriously, and the aircraft soon rolled out on schedule. Better yet, fewer discrepancies were recorded under my watch, and I was nominated to be the base's airman of the month. That opened the door to a new opportunity and a promotion to sergeant. I was charged with managing the ground equipment section. This group had a bad reputation for being filthy, but nobody working there seemed to care. I accepted the offer to oversee that section and went to work turning it completely around.

The first thing I did was to get rid of two airmen who always seemed to be soaked in oil, which created a serious fire hazard not only for themselves, but the rest of the hangar crew as well. That action caught the attention of the remaining three airmen. They quickly shaped up and worked harder to ensure the section was neat, orderly and hazard-free in a very short period of time.

That section became my pride and joy. It was also another feather in my cap in attracting attention from my supervisors who really wanted me to volunteer to extend my enlistment. However, I didn't jump at that opportunity. That turned out to be an incredibly wise decision because my unit shipped off to Vietnam just three months later.

While in the U.S. Air Force, my extra-curricular activities involved working as a bartender, managing a service station, racing stockcars and, my favorite, chasing women. As my initial enlistment ended, I decided I had invested enough time in the military, and it was time to pursue a bigger dream, even if I didn't know what that was at the time.

Time for training and fun

At the end of October 1966, I returned to Wisconsin where I got a job temporarily working at the same feed mill. Yet, I was still dreaming big, especially about a career in aviation. I wanted to continue training as an aircraft mechanic by attending one of nation's elite aviation technical schools.

I called the McDonald-Douglas representative I worked with at Wurtsmith Air Force Base. He recommended three schools: Spartan,

Embry Riddle, and Northrop Institute. I picked Northrop because it was based in southern California. Today, I serve on the tech committee at Spartan.

I applied to the Northrop Institute of Technology in Inglewood, Calif., where I hoped to pursue certification working on jet airframes and aviation power plants, which is a fancy way of describing an engine. The money I earned at the mill, when combined with the Veterans Administration education benefit I earned for my military service, helped ensure that I'd have a great send off to the Golden State. I was twenty-two years old when I moved to California. Once there, I joined a class of fifty-five students, of which only twelve graduated. I found classes to be relatively easy and wound up graduating third in my class despite working my way through school.

Prior to enrolling at Northrop, I sold my car, motorcycle, and pickup truck. The cash came in handy for paying for my room and meals. It also eliminated a few things that could tempt me to go astray. Upon arrival in Inglewood, I applied to work as a bartender for Shakey's Pizza Parlor. Because it was located right next to the school, that made it convenient to manage work and school commitments.

It was a great deal! I received a good wage; plus, tips and all the free pizza and Mojos I could eat. After two months, I was promoted to head bartender. I soon discovered that I could trade a pizza with bartenders at Mother's Bar next door in exchange for free beer. Eventually, that bar hired me to be a bouncer when I wasn't working at Shakey's. That brought in even more money!

For a young single guy, life was great. I was also so busy attending classes during the day and working at night that I didn't have to get into any real trouble, not that I needed any temptation to go astray. My experience at Northrop Institute seemed long at the time, but thanks to my jobs at Shakey's and Mother's Bar, the time passed quickly.

Living in California really was a different way of life than I was used to when I lived Wisconsin and Michigan. But, I foolishly opted to leave the sunshine behind and move back to the Midwest. Yes, I really did miss the snow. I found a job working for Northwest Airlines in St. Paul, Minn., the summer of 1968. The position involved fixing jets, performing aircraft inspections, and recording maintenance completed on Boeing 707, Boeing 727 and Lockheed L-188 Electra aircraft.

However, compared to my time in California, I wasn't living life anymore. I was pretty much just a number at Northwest Airlines, and I wasn't used to that. I supervised the de-icing crew, and was quickly reminded that although I like snow, I truly hated winter.

It wasn't long after the first winter storms hit the area that I found myself outside with my crew in biting-cold weather spraying liquid de-icer on jets in below-freezing temperatures. I began to reminisce about the good times I enjoyed in California. I came out of the hangar one night and couldn't find my car because it was buried in snow.

I was griping to my father about the situation one day, and he gave me the best possible advice he could have offered. "Bob," he said, "the best time to move is when all your personal belongings fit in the trunk of your car."

It didn't take long for me to realize he was absolutely right. So, I gave my notice to Northwest Airlines, packed my car, and headed back to the California sun.

Chapter 4

High school photos

My brother, Stan, and I before school in 1958.

Pete DeBoer with his 1937 Pontiac that he bought for $40.

Al Wiersma, Randy Hiama and me in my first car, which I bought when I was just 15 years old.

Al Wiersma and Randy Hiama in front of my first car.

My mother and father, Ruby and Rink, coming home from Old Mexico around 1961.

My 4-H club at the state gathering. I'm third from the right in the back row.

My basketball team in 1958. I'm in the front right wearing jersey No. 9.

Practicing my free-throws during my freshman year in 1959.

My stock and road car racing days at Wilbur Speedway.

An advertisement from the local paper promoting one of the races in which I competed.

Chapter 5

Becoming a flight engineer

Great teammates who became lifelong friends, the three of us flew dignitaries and starlets around the globe. Don Short, left, served as the pilot of the Gulfstream II, I was the flight engineer, and Ed Hahn, our co-pilot.

My first month back in California was spent celebrating my return and feebly looking for work. Fortunately, Rajay Turbochargers, in Long Beach, which was a small aircraft turbocharger manufacturer, hired me as an inspector. However, I had only been at that job for a few weeks when a representative of Northrop Corporation called out of the blue to ask if I would be interested in being a flight engineer on their recently-purchased Gulfstream II corporate jet.

I interviewed with the president of the company and with Don Short, a pilot who flew Air Force One for President Lyndon Johnson. When I returned to work the next day, I learned that Northrop had already called my boss, who handed me a paycheck for the entire week and directed me to report to Northrop the next day. I processed into Northrop that Friday, received another paycheck and a ticket to Savannah, Ga., to watch the new Gulfstream jet being built at the Grumman plant. The plane had serial No. 42, and it was the first Gulfstream to ever receive an FAA 135.2 air taxi certificate.

Back then, a flight engineer was an essential position onboard any aircraft. He was responsible for checking the aircraft's systems before takeoff, including everything from hydraulics to air conditioning. The engineer also ensured the aircraft was properly balanced by ensuring the weight of passengers and baggage was properly distributed and would not shift during flight.

During takeoff, the engineer would monitor an array of gauges and indicators recording engine performance, lighting, and flight controls. He was responsible for troubleshooting any problems during flight because the pilots could not take their hands or eyes off the controls. Upon landing, the engineer would complete a post-flight inspection and schedule the aircraft for any necessary or routine maintenance. If that wasn't enough, on a corporate jet, the flight engineer also served as the cabin steward. He would greet passengers, help store luggage, serve beverages and snacks, pick up trash, and ensure everyone was comfortable.

Pilots often get credit for navigating an aircraft from Point A to Point B, but it was really the flight engineer who ensured a jet was fully-operational, and all systems were working properly.

While in Savannah, I also had the opportunity to attend classes about the jet I'd be overseeing. Watching the assembly line and learning about all the planning required to produce a complete aircraft was an education all by itself. As you can imagine, the attention to detail that goes into building a jet is incredible. "Close enough," is not something you'll ever hear on a jet assembly line.

This was the first of a long list of professional courses I would need to attend to prepare me for my new job. The schools were scattered throughout the United States and Canada. Fortunately, I loved to travel!

To get ready to work as a flight engineer, I had to leave Savannah for Canada to learn about the Rolls-Royce Spey engine that powered the Gulfstream II jet. From there, I flew to Pittsburg to learn how to set up a corporate flight maintenance department, and how to serve as a personal steward aboard a private jet owned by U.S. Steel Corporation. For two weeks, I learned the ins and outs of catering to dignitaries. Steward training is acquired only by experience, and it involves a lot more than just learning how to pour coffee for pilots and passengers.

Back then, the idea of using private jets to shuttle executives and very important people was considered a novelty. Northrop's guests often included top-level corporate executives, foreign dignitaries, government officials, politicians, celebrities, and other highly-influential people. As part of my training, I took several flights with U.S. Steel executives aboard one of their corporate aircraft. Each flight was unique due to its destination and passenger roster. At the end of this book, there are two lists showing the names of luminaries and celebrities whom I had the honor of shuttling to various destinations aboard the Gulfstream II.

Next, I returned to California to learn about the Gulfstream II's navigation system for a few weeks before making a quick jaunt to Phoenix for training on auxiliary power units. When all my training was complete, so was the aircraft, and I returned to Los Angeles just in time for initial flight testing. There were no textbooks available to teach me how to be a good flight engineer. So, I kept a lot of notes and later used them to write a manual for crew members employed by Northrop to train those who may be hired in the future.

After completing my flight engineer training, I was scheduled to accompany all test pilot training flights and record any discrepancies I noticed. My reports were reviewed to see if I missed anything in my observations. I felt like I was on probation during this acceptance period, which seemed to last a long time. It wasn't too difficult because, if any mechanical difficulty arose, then I could rely on local representatives from the Grumman and AiResearch corporations for their knowledge and advice. Through that experience, I learned the importance of knowing who to call when problems came up, when to ask for information, and what details to seek. That would prove to be invaluable later when I was fully responsible for overseeing my own flights.

I knew it would be impossible to memorize all the small details I would need to retain, but I did create a personal directory of experts whom I could rely upon to answer any questions, and give me information I needed. It was a skill that paid off throughout my career. Knowing who to call for whatever reason can be applied to any type of business, and that skill is ranked as one of the most important lessons I learned.

On my own

My first operational trip for Northrop was with Thomas V. Jones, who was president of the company and chairman of the board. We were expected to fly to Altoona, Pa., and back to Los Angeles. The flight out was flawless, and all the preflight tests for the return trip checked out okay. However, the engine wouldn't start when we were ready to depart. Both pilots and Mr. Jones automatically turned to me to ask, "What's wrong, Bob?"

What a position to be in on my first trip as the official flight engineer! But, it turned out to be one of the most important lessons I would learn on that job. First, I had to convince myself not to panic because I was scared to death of the responsibility upon my shoulders. I had nobody else to turn to for advice. Then, I recalled my previous trouble-shooting experiences, and that brought several things to mind. I knew to get the facts, organize ideas, and then proceed with a plan. But, I knew I had to keep an open mind in case any new information came to light.

Fortunately, I had the foresight to place a few spare parts onboard the aircraft prior to leaving Los Angeles. Those were the parts needed to get us up and running again. How I handled that situation gave me the confidence I needed in myself, and assured the company president that his firm made the right choice in hiring me.

Memorable people and experiences

As I continued flying for the next eight years, I enjoyed a variety of memorable experiences. For example, in 1969, I was proud to be an American when the first Boeing 747 arrived at the Paris Airshow.

During my time as a flight engineer, I visited thirty-five countries that had purchased F-5 fighter jets from Northrop. We flew to air bases in the Atlantic region in June 1969 and the Pacific in November of that year. We flew around the world in each direction.

When corporate executives weren't using the jet for business, the company rented it out to other people. I spent anywhere from a single day up to a month in some places. I felt special being in the background as important corporate business meetings were conducted while we were in flight. I found it insightful to observe how each of the executives approached their responsibilities, as well as their leadership styles for motivating others or holding them accountable. It was not part of my job description to listen to conversations, but I'm glad I did. Learning from those incredible leaders positioned me to run my own company many years later.

I fixed that plane everywhere in the world. One time, I had to replace two windshields in a rainstorm while visiting Rio de Janeiro. I had to work 40 hours straight to keep everyone on schedule. In that instance, the plane had been rented by Justin Dart. He was a superb entrepreneur who ran Rexall Drug Stores, and also owned Duracell battery company, West Bend housewares and the Hobart restaurant supply firm. Eventually, he sold all those firms to Kraft and became that company's CEO.

Mr. Dart was so grateful for my effort to maintain the schedule that he invited me to join his staff on a cruise along the Amazon River during the jet's next stop. Despite having worked nearly two days without rest, I jumped at the opportunity. However, while navigating down the piranha-infested waters, the boat's engine broke down. After a rather lengthy delay, Mr. Dart suggested that I go below to assist the ship's crew in diagnosing the problem. Within a few minutes of entering the engine room, which really was a fire hazard with grease and oil all over the place, the engine fired up. When I emerged from the engine room, I got a standing ovation despite never having picked up a wrench. However, I graciously accepted the applause.

Everyone wanted to rent our plane because we were the first company to use a Gulfstream II jet. Before that, Lear jets were popular private air taxis. At many places we visited, I thought it was funny that people kept asking if our Gulfstream was a Learjet.

The first paying customer aboard the Gulfstream II was Howard Hughes, who needed to be picked up following an earthquake in Nicaragua and shuttled to Canada. We also shuttled several World War II fighter aces on a trip to the Orient, including Johnny Alison, David Lee "Tex" Hill, and Charlie Bond. We even flew Mohammad Reza Pahlavi, who was the Shaw of Iran until he was overthrown in 1979. That was an interesting experience requiring additional training in protocol to learn not to touch the dignitary. For example, an aide would take the Shaw's coat and pass it to me, and I would hang it up.

America's first air taxi

The idea of owning a private jet was unusual when I worked as a flight engineer. So, it was more efficient and cost-effective for executives and entertainers to rent Northrop's aircraft to travel. The jet provided a decent business atmosphere, and saved passengers hours of travel time.

It was a tough economic time for America and Northrop wanted to show prospective buyers that the Gulfstream II could be rented out as a taxi to help offset the cost of ownership. Besides, commercial air travel proved to be so hard on executives and entertainers that it often left them drained of energy before important meetings, major presentations, or big performances. Renting out the Gulfstream II was a smart move on Northrop's part because, rather than incurring 100 percent of the financial burden of owning and maintaining the aircraft, leasing jet time became a profitable endeavor.

Our aircraft became the first official Gulfstream air taxi in the United States. Achieving that designation was no easy task. There were a number of hoops to jump through to get the air taxi certificate. Then, just as soon as we determined we had complied with all the regulations, the Federal Aviation Administration created a few more.

I became the Gulfstream II's chief inspector. I had to personally inspect the jet after each flight, note any problems, schedule maintenance, and maintain a constant log of where the jet was located at any time. I also noted who was on board, where it was headed, how long it stayed, and just about everything else except what the pilot had for breakfast. Once we attained the air taxi certification, it meant we were flying more often to shuttle a new group of famous people and executives.

Within a year, I became the director of maintenance who was responsible for coordinating service with various repair facilities around the world. I was now responsible for procuring parts and supervising mechanics. The workload became so heavy that I elected to give up the director of maintenance title so that I could focus solely on flying. That decision allowed me to return to a position I truly enjoyed, which was serving our passengers. Some of the newly-hired staff had allowed our service standards to slide, and Northrop wanted to ensure the company provided first-class service to its high-paying clients.

Some of the other distinguished guests I had the privilege to shuttle around the globe included:

- Reza Pahlavi, the crown prince of Iran.

- Prince Bernhard of Lippe-Biesterfeld, otherwise known as Prince

Bernhard of the Netherlands.

- Howard Hughes, once the richest man in the world, who founded the Hughes Aircraft Company. His firm manufactured some of the fastest aircraft of its time. He later acquired Trans World Airlines and Air West.

- Lucille Ball, a famous actress who warmed the hearts of families for many years as the red-headed comedienne in a variety of TV shows. She was also the first woman to run a major TV studio that produced shows like *Star Trek* and *Mission Impossible*.

- Sonny and Cher, who were dynamic entertainers in the 1960s and 1970s. Sonny went on to become mayor of Palm Springs, and was elected to Congress as a representative. Cher, the "Goddess of Pop," worked as a singer, actress, and entertainer worldwide, and still is to this day.

- The "Rat Pack" of Dean Martin, Frank Sinatra, Peter Lawford, Joey Bishop and Sammy Davis, Jr.

- Elvis Presley, the "King of Rock and Roll."

- Ronald Reagan, when he was governor of California.

- Musician Rod Stewart.

- The rock band *Chicago*.

I have a vivid memory of spending the night of my 27th birthday singing gospel songs with Elvis in the legendary entertainer's hotel suite at the Las Vegas Hilton. Our crew shuttled Elvis to events so often that the plane was featured several times in the documentary movie *Elvis on Tour*. Elvis was a genuinely nice man, and a very interesting person with whom to have a conversation. For some reason, he really liked the service I provided. One time, he had his company send me a $100 check. That would be the equivalent of a $650 tip in 2023.

Elvis on Tour wasn't the Gulfstream II's only media exposure. The jet made an appearance in the movie *Disappearance of Flight 412, which* starred Glen Ford. Our Gulfstream II could also be seen taking off each week in the opening segment of the TV show *Hart to Hart.* A clip of that scene can be found at https://youtu.be/AbZaiQWe03U. I felt sorry for the cameraman who was capturing that scene because our pilot calculated the exact position on the runway where the plane would take off. We were so close to him when we left the ground that he may have been burned by our exhaust.

The Gulfstream II held such fond memories for me that when the aircraft's interior was redesigned, I acquired all the seats and kept them in storage for nearly 45 years. A few years ago, I acquired a 1972 Econoline van with 72,000 miles on it. I gutted the interior and rebuilt it using the original chairs and galley from our jet. I still get a kick out of taking that van to car shows because everyone wants to sit in the same chairs Elvis, and Sonny and Cher sat in when they were at the peak of their careers.

Chapter 6

Product support years

Me enjoying a cruise along the Amazon River during a trip with Justin Dart, owner of Dart Industries and, later, Kraft Foods.

After my son, Ryan, was born, I decided to stop flying so I could spend more time at home. He was crawling when I left on a trip to Iran, but walking when I returned five weeks later. It showed me how much I was missing by being away from home so often and so long. I made up my mind that I didn't want to fly anymore.

I loved the job, the people I served as passengers, and the people I worked with all over the world. But, when I decided to give up flying, I was emotionally done. I no longer had enthusiasm for the position, and it weighed on me whenever I was gone. There were some regular passengers who really wished I would continue to escort them on trips, but I just lost passion for that aspect of my job.

I also realized I was giving up a lot of other opportunities just because I was traveling so much. Each year I had been flying, several people requested that I transfer to their departments or, if they rented the jet, that I come to work at their companies. When I expressed interest, they would follow-up with a formal interview. But, something would always happen to cause the opportunity to simply evaporate. I never understood why because initially they were so excited about having me come to work for them, and that enthusiasm grew during the interviews. But, then I wouldn't hear anything about the job and, eventually, similar offers stopped coming. It was as though people were no longer interested in having me work for them.

I thought that was strange, until Robert Elder, a retired Navy admiral and senior board member with the Northrop Corporation, provided some insight to the situation. He explained that Thomas V. Jones, the president of Northrop, had put word out that I was off limits. After Mr. Jones learned I interviewed for another position, he would put an end to any attempts to transfer me to a different job.

Apparently, Mr. Jones appreciated how well I served his wife, Ruth, whenever she would accompany us on a trip. I often escorted her wherever she wanted to go. Mr. and Mrs. Jones had such high respect for me and my professionalism that they didn't want to lose me. However, Robert's explanation opened my eyes to the fact I was never going to advance further in my career as long as I worked for Northrop as a flight engineer.

I started sniffing around for opportunities outside of Northrop. One day, I was flying to South America with Welko Gasich, who was the vice president of Northrop's Aircraft Division, and his wife, Pat. He asked if I would ever consider working for his division, but I explained the situation to him. He really sympathized with my desire to spend more time at home with my wife and young son.

"You don't have to leave Northrop," said Mr. Gasich. "I will hire you in my division. I'm not scared of Mr. Jones! Consider this your last trip as a flight engineer."

He got the ball rolling and, a few weeks later, I was flying again with Mr. and Mrs. Jones. Shortly after taking off, I made him a cup of his favorite Earl Gray tea and took it back to him in the cabin. As I approached, he put down his paper and said, "So, you're leaving us." Until then, he had been giving me a kind of cool reception. I told him, "Yes, sir. I am moving over to product support to answer maintenance questions about F-5s that Northrop's technicians may have in the field." We talked for a few moments, and then he simply said, "Well, you're going to have to tell Mrs. Jones."

Fortunately, she was very understanding, and they both wished me well in my new endeavor. That was literally my final trip as a flight engineer.

I know Mr. Jones really appreciated me as an employee because I ensured that his plane was ready to fly whenever he wanted to go somewhere. All the years we flew together, I never left him stranded anywhere. I also got to know the other executives fairly well, too. I maintained a personal log about what they liked to eat and drink so that I could have that ready for them after we took off. I took very good care of all my passengers, especially the ones I flew with regularly.

I liked flying and serving aboard the Gulfstream II, but being with my children as they grew up was far more important. I could always return to flying when the children were older, but they needed me at that point in their lives.

A new career in product support

On my first day in the new position, Jim Young, the senior engineer, asked what aircraft systems I felt comfortable supporting. I told him I could work on anything except guns. So, he assigned me to provide product support for aircraft engines and hydraulic systems, such as landing gear.

My colleagues worked hard, but liked to have fun, too. In fact, the second day I came to work, I found my desk chair wound down as close to the ground as it could go. Then, the next day, Vern Twyman and Skip Davies, wound my chair all the way up as far as it would go. Another time, they rigged my desk drawer with rubber bands so that when I opened it, the drawer would snap back and slam shut throwing my things all over the desk. They really made me feel welcome, and I became close friends with several of those coworkers.

It was a desk job for which I was pretty much confined to an office. But, I had fixed work hours, and I was home every night. All my work was done via the phone. So, whenever technicians had problems they couldn't solve by themselves, they would speak to me. I would either help them troubleshoot the issue, or advise them on how to resolve the problem.

Before I could settle into the job, I had to take more advanced training on the F-5 and its various components. Because of my background, it didn't take a lot of time for me to get up to speed on how the system operated. Surprisingly, the Gulfstream II was a more complex aviation system than the F-5. Because they must be battle-ready at all times, military jets are generally more straightforward to understand, and easier to maintain.

I also worked as a liaison with other departments. If there was a problem I couldn't help resolve, I would consult with engineering quality control or other senior technicians to iron out the situation. We'd work together to develop a solution that I could put back in the hands of our tech reps. The field technicians were very appreciative of our assistance because they were often on the flight line all by themselves.

Every air force base around the world which had an F-5 fighter in its inventory also had at least one Northrop technician tasked with keeping the jet operational, and ready to use. The jets were located in thirty-five countries. The F-5s may have been on U.S. Air Force bases or used by the armed forces of America's allies.

I was fortunate to have been able to meet most of those technicians when I was flying around the world in the Gulfstream II. As representatives of Northrop, it was important that we were very good to the technicians because our company's reputation was based on their ability to keep our planes flying. It was essential that we keep those technicians happy and feeling well-supported.

Occasionally, I would get to work with U.S.-based technicians in the field. For example, I would visit Nellis Air Force Base in Las Vegas because of its proximity to our Los Angeles office. I would help them run what's called a test cell where an engine is put through its paces in a repair facility. That way technicians could evaluate the engine's performance while the jet is on the ground. The engine itself is mounted on a stand. While it's operating at full speed, a technician can adjust how air flows through the engine, and make other changes to how it's operating.

It's a hair-raising experience, to say the least. When you're running an engine at full bore while tweaking airflow as its afterburner turns red hot—and you're sitting one foot away—that will get your attention, especially if you think something is going to come apart.

If technicians were having a problem diagnosing a particular issue with an engine, then that would fall into my area of expertise. If we couldn't solve the problem during a series of phone calls, I would need to fly out and offer assistance on site. I always tried to provide excellent customer service to our technicians in the field because I knew people were badgering them with questions related to the aircraft's operational readiness. The last thing anyone wanted was a service problem to wind up sitting on someone's desk for days without a resolution.

So, as soon as I received an inquiry from a technician, I would immediately respond that I received the message, and promised to reply soon with an update. Then, after I spoke with someone in engineering, I would respond again either with the information needed to correct a problem or with assurance that we were taking action to get it resolved. I wanted the technicians to know the problem was in our hands, and that I would be closely monitoring the situation. My bosses in product support liked that, too, because they had confidence that nothing would ever be overlooked.

I would provide a status update every few days or every week, depending upon the situation. That way technicians and their bosses would know we had not dropped the ball. Back in those days, it was unusual for technicians to receive a follow up message, even to ensure their inquiry had been received, and was being addressed. Not only was that unfair to technicians in the field, but our lack of quick support reflected poorly on Northrop. So, I worked hard to keep those lines of communication open and active.

Whenever our customer needed a jet fixed, it was essential that everyone at Northrop come together to support our client. It was my job to ensure the solution was found, and quickly conveyed to technicians completing the repair. It was a great environment to work in because it required a strong team effort in order for everyone to be successful.

Jim Young's guidance

While I worked in product support, I had the great privilege of working with Jim Young. He was the lead engineer on our team. When it came to writing reports, he truly held me accountable by proofreading everything I sent out. He took the time to teach me how to write properly, and it's a skill that helped me greatly throughout my career.

Back in high school, I had a crazy English teacher who was more concerned whether I had a pencil in my pocket than if I could write well. In fact, she gave me an F for the day or zeros on a project simply because I didn't follow her rule about having a pencil. As a result, I really didn't learn how to communicate well in high school, but Jim changed that.

Whenever I was going to send a response to a technician, Jim would review it first. I'd get my drafts back all marked up to the point I basically had to rewrite it from scratch. But, Jim would help me organize my thoughts, and ensure I was using proper grammar and spelling. By ensuring my reports flowed properly, he did more than anyone else to help me become a better writer. Thanks to Jim, I was able to publish several magazine articles which helped establish me as an expert on jet engines and aircraft window repair.

Building a network

When I was working as a flight engineer on the Gulfstream II, little did I know that the informal network I was building throughout the world would become so important to my product support role, and absolutely essential to the success of a business I would eventually start.

When I was shuttling Northrop executives around the globe, after we would land and taxi to wherever we needed to go, the passengers would get off, and talk about airplane business. Perhaps the customer wanted to purchase more aircraft, or they were shopping for jets to buy. While they conducted their meetings, I would perform a walk-around inspection of the Gulfstream II and take care of anything that needed to be addressed before the executives were ready to leave.

Generally, I had my work finished within an hour or two. Then, I had to find things to do to occupy my time. I would always try to locate the airport's tech rep for the Northrop Corporation. I really didn't need anything, but just wanted to meet that person to either introduce myself or shore up an established relationship. I would personally get to know anyone doing mechanical work on the Gulfstream. However, the tech rep would often introduce me to other people on the flight line, whether they worked for Northrop, the airport, or some other aviation company.

I would also meet flight engineers who flew in with other companies. Perhaps they were shuttling people in for a golf outing or social visit, or they were in the area for business as well. Either way, we would all hang out watching television or just shooting the breeze in the break room waiting for our passengers to return. After flying on the Gulfstream II for so long, I literally had hundreds of friendships in many countries. I got to know about their families, hobbies, career goals, and just about everything else during the time we chatted before having to leave again.

Like me, many other flight engineers had ambitions to move up in their careers. Many of them became the directors of maintenance at different facilities around the world. Even though we didn't communicate directly after they moved on, I could put a face to a name. They knew me, and I knew them. We exchanged business cards, and kept in touch if I was ever in their area. I always knew where they were working. So, when I started my own business, I sent them all my company's first promotional brochure. I had an informal network of hundreds of people involved in aircraft maintenance all over America and the world.

Diagnosing nose gear failure

One of the problems I helped to correct involved a major issue with the F-5 nose gear. When an aircraft needed to be towed, a tug vehicle was hooked up to the nose gear. The technician was supposed to disconnect the steering actuator before pulling on the unit, but that didn't always happen. As a result, the center shaft of the steering actuator would break.

The damage wasn't always obvious because the actuator would break about three-quarters of the way through the shaft. The plane could still move; however, a cracked actuator severely compromises the ability to control an aircraft on the ground. When a pilot would climb aboard the jet and start speeding down the runway, any vibration would crack it the rest of the way. That caused the nose wheel to spin sideways. Eventually, the gear would simply fold, and the jet's nose would plow into the runway, creating a very dangerous situation.

If a pilot was fortunate enough to get airborne before the actuator cracked completely, then it would certainly collapse upon landing. Getting this problem fixed was a big priority for Northrop because several F-5s had been destroyed. I worked with the engineers and tech crew to implement a simple solution. We put little plates on the side of the landing gear where a tow tug would be attached. When the steering actuator was disconnected, the plates would drop out of the way to expose where the tug should be attached to the aircraft.

That way, technicians could not inadvertently hook up a tow bar to an aircraft while the steering actuator was still engaged. There was no way for an aircraft to be towed, even on purpose, with the actuator still engaged. A technician would have to disengage the actuator, tow the vehicle wherever it needed to go, and then re-engage the actuator.

The solution worked so well that I helped write an article for *Technical Services*, a magazine distributed to Northrop owners and technicians worldwide, explaining how we corrected the problem. It was the first time I had an opportunity to write an article for publication.

Solving an engine problem

I was involved in troubleshooting another problem involving the F-5. There was a linkage issue between the engine, and the aircraft's frame. It required me to work with General Electric engineers to develop a solution.

The situation was complicated by the fact it required working with people outside of Northrop. The Northrop engineers would say it was an engine problem that should be fixed by General Electric, because that firm built the engine. However, GE engineers claimed it was an aircraft problem that should be fixed by Northrop, because our company built the F-5.

There was a lot of finger-pointing going on between the two companies as engineers on both sides butted heads. Finally, I stepped in to remind everyone that it wasn't an engine problem or an aircraft problem, but "our" problem. We needed to engineer a fix because it involved "our" airplane. The solution would require Northrop and General Electric to work together to help our mutual customer.

I orchestrated some meetings between workers at both companies to brainstorm solutions. We discovered the source of the problem, and it rested in how the throttle in the cockpit communicated with the engine to direct fuel flow. There was a linkage that transferred data between the airframe and engine, and the two components weren't speaking in the same language. It turned out to be a minor problem that was easily corrected, but it just required both teams to come together to support the same customer.

Promotion to senior customer relations rep

In 1976, I was promoted to the position of senior customer relations representative. The F-5 had been around for many years, and the T-38 had been in production even longer. Now the company was modifying the aircraft into an F-5G, which was later renamed the F-20. Sleeker and faster, the new aircraft utilized one engine. Since I was already known around Northrop as the "engine man," I was tasked to work with a team to install the engine onto a new jet.

When the project was completed, I was reassigned to a role that helped sell the F-5G aircraft to potential buyers. It was my job to take really good care of foreign dignitaries, politicians, military leaders, and other VIPs touring the plant. They needed to be wined and dined, and I wound up going to dinner with a number of them.

However, nobody bought the new jet. Mr. Jones even tried offering the National Guard free maintenance for ten years, but there still weren't any takers. Northrop had a lot of competition at the time. The company was also releasing the YF-17, which had dual General Electric 404 engines in it. When flying, it was a fabulous airplane—a real screamer.

The way project contracts were written at that time, the winning bidder was awarded the entire contract. For example, if 100 planes were needed, then one company would get to build all 100 jets. Contacts were not awarded in a way that allowed two firms to share responsibility for building the same model jets. Because all the planes were made by one firm, that's why the same F-100 engine was used on the F-15 and F-16. However, the Air Force was having major turbine problems with the F-100 engines on the F-15 aircraft. In fact, half of the jets were grounded at one point due to turbine problems.

There weren't enough airplanes in inventory to justify rebuilding the turbine section on F-100 engines, and that stacked the deck against Northrop to receive a winner-take-all contract. The Navy told Northrop it could build any airplane the company wanted to build, as long as it had two engines. As a result, Northrop's YF-17 aircraft lost the competition, and the contract to build the F-18 was awarded to McDonald Douglas. That company added 1,360 pounds of additional landing gear on the jets so they could land on aircraft carriers. Those jets were still flying in 2023.

Overseeing international co-production

To help sell more aircraft internationally, Northrop would offer incentives under what was called an offset program. A country would put in an order for aircraft and, in return, Northrop would allow a piece of the airplane, like a wing tip, to be manufactured in that country. The nation could apply the cost to produce that component to offset the total purchase price of a new aircraft. It was a win-win for Northrop because the company sold more aircraft, and the countries which purchased them enjoyed an ownership stake in the jet's production.

I was appointed to be the manager of international quality assurance for co-production. I knew a lot of people throughout Northrop. One of my good friends, Steve Perry, also worked as a flight engineer on the Gulfstream II. He eventually oversaw the assembly line to build Northrop's YF-17 and F-18 aircraft. However, because Northrop only produced about 40 percent of the F-18s, Steve needed a top-notch person to oversee quality control, and I was selected for the job.

It was a challenge to gather parts being manufactured all over the world and get them to the Northrop assembly plant. In order for the program to be successful, all the parts had to conform to Northrop specifications. The company wouldn't release anything unless it passed my quality control process. It was a very important job, as well as the final position I held at the company.

Because of my background in aviation, there was some type of quality assurance component to my job responsibilities in every position I held. So, the job was a natural fit for me, but it required me to take on a tremendous amount of responsibility. I supervised a team of quality assurance inspectors around the globe. I also had to be on my game when it came to corporate politics, especially because so many people from different countries were involved.

Each country that flew F-5 aircraft had a designated program manager to oversee Northrop's interests in that country. I remember one country's manager was giving me a hard time. He claimed that it was too expensive for his department to keep my quality assurance person on his team. So, he tried to cut the inspector's hours. As diplomatically as possible, I explained that if he couldn't justify the cost of having a full-time quality assurance inspector, then I could not allow the parts my employee was inspecting to be shipped to that country. That irritated the program manager, and he escalated the situation to Welko Gasich, the vice president of Northrop's Aviation Division.

Fortunately, Mr. Gasich explained that if I was holding up a shipment, then I had every right to do so because my inspector's hours were being cut to save some money. Well, after that, the program manager relented, my inspector had his work hours restored, and our parts were shipped to the country.

The purpose of a quality assurance program is to ensure that all parts are produced to Northrop's exact standards, and installed the way Northrop dictates that it be done. That is the only way to ensure an aircraft will work as intended. It's rather foolish to try to save a few dollars by scaling back the inspection process when lives and multi-million-dollar aircraft were at stake just because a part was made wrong or poorly installed.

I liked the job because it allowed me to be somewhat flexible in my schedule. As I was developing my aircraft window business, I could sneak away to visit Los Angeles International Airport to evaluate a business jet and give its owner an estimate for repairing the aircraft's windows. My secretary at Northrop would take messages for me, and relay that information when I returned to the office.

I really didn't have that flexibility when I was working in customer relations. I could not be in the middle of a VIP tour escorting the secretary of some country's air force around the plant, or taking him to lunch, and then excuse myself for an hour to work on my aircraft window repair business. Typically, I could only work on my business after hours or on weekends. But, in quality assurance, as long as I got my work done, and I ensured that I made up the hours at Northrop, then I could slip away for a short time.

Back to school

As I was overseeing quality assurance and starting my business on the side from 1979 to 1982, I was also taking night classes at Redlands University in Redlands, Calif., to complete my bachelor's degree in business administration.

This is also when Jim Young's patience in helping me to become a better writer really started to pay off. I often received good grades on the papers I submitted. In fact, the university requested that I allow one of my term papers to be used as an example for other students to follow when writing their own research papers.

It had been a while since I was in a classroom for anything other than a few days or a week of specific technical training. I received a two-year diploma from Northrop University in airframes and powerplants (A&P) in 1967, and that qualified me to get my official aviation maintenance technician license from the FAA. With that, I was authorized to perform maintenance, repairs, and tests on aircraft and various components.

The business degree I earned from Redlands University really helped prepare me for the next chapter of my life. That next step would alter the course of my destiny after I became a small business owner.

Chapter 7

Photos from my Northrop years

Me visiting my brother, Stan, left, at his home in Madison, Wis.

Me visiting my brother-in-law, George Levey.

Sporting my first and only beard when serving as a bartender at Shakey's Pizza in Inglewood, Calif.

Me holding the largest fish I ever caught, a Pompano,
off the coast of Florida. The other man was our guide,
whose name I don't remember.

Dave Crettol, right, and me during the 1975 rolllout of Northrop's F-20 Tigershark light fighter jet.

As Northrop's senior customer relations representative, my job was to escort visiting dignitaries around the plant. Here I am showing our latest F-20 Tigershark light fighter jet to two members of the Argentinan air force.

*Our Gulfstream II aircraft parked in front of the
Northrop hangar located at Hawthorne Municipal Airport
in Hawthorne, Calif.*

*The original interior of the Gulfstream II, for which I served
as flight engineer for tail number N8000-J. Later, I was
able to acquire those seats and incorporate them into a van
I redesigned. People loved sitting in the same seats so many
celebrities did aboard the jet.*

Our Gulfstream II team, from left, Pilot Don Short, Copilot Ed Hahn and me, the flight engineer.

Chapter 8

Pursuing my own business

This photo of the interior of the Aircraft Window Repairs shop shows where our technicians work to save aircraft owners money by refurbishing windows and lenses.

In 1982, I had to leave Northrop because I was working too many hours in my garage at night fixing aircraft windows. I was burning the candle on both ends and could feel the stress. I loved my job as the international quality assurance manager for Northrop, but it was quickly becoming very obvious that I had stumbled upon a terrific need within the aviation industry. That was to help companies greatly reduce costs by repairing aircraft windows, rather than replacing them.

However, embarking upon this unique business opportunity quickly created a new set of challenges. The first was the FAA would not certify the garage at my home as a repair center. So, I needed to buy some industrial space. I found a 4,000-square-foot building which I thought would be more than enough to complete all the repair work. In fact, I rented out 2,500 square feet to another company because I thought there was no way I would ever need that much space.

We outgrew that space within eighteen months because everyone and his brother was sending windows to us. Aircraft Window Repairs (AWR) was the only FAA-certified repair station for windows anywhere in the world. We had so many windows waiting to be repaired that we stacked them in the parking lot and secured a repair order to the pile with a brick. There was no room in the facility to store windows and be able to repair them.

I bought a much larger facility two doors down from the initial location in 1985, and we still fix windows from that building in Torrance, Calif. It is about four miles from Zamperini Field, a general aviation airport operated by the City of Torrance. It was relatively convenient for people to fly in and deliver or pick up windows. We also had a lot of windows arrive by truck.

Fortunately, the city took my original property by eminent domain in order to install a water well at that location. I received $550,000 for it, which I considered to be a reasonable sum for the property because it gave me a significant down payment for the new location. Ironically, when the city started drilling for water, they discovered it was so polluted that it could not be cleaned. I would have thought someone would have tested the water quality before insisting on taking control of the land, but it worked out well for us.

I would have liked to keep the original building and dedicate it exclusively to fixing windows for the U.S. Air Force. But, without that space, I had to shut down the project. I needed every inch of our new 6,000-square-foot building to store and repair all the windows we received for corporate jets. The first property has remained empty since the city acquired it in 1985. If property hasn't been used by government within 20 years of being acquired by eminent domain, there is a rule allowing me to buy it back for whatever sum I originally received. But, I haven't explored that option yet.

Speaking engagements

To promote Aircraft Window Repairs, I traveled the country doing presentations at conventions from the 1990s until recently. I spoke at the 2018 National Business Aviation Association (NBAA) conference in Orlando, the 2019 Southern California Professional Aviation Maintenance Association (SCPAMA) meeting, and the 2022 Minnesota Aviation Conference, to name a few.

I enjoyed presenting and speaking with potential customers in order to get people to look at our windows, and not just through them. We developed a very good reputation because we adhere to the system I set up. We never have reworks or warranty work. I think that is a good testimony to the quality of work my company provides.

I was invited by the Professional Aviation Maintenance Association (PAMA), Westchester Aircraft Maintenance Association (WAMA) and the National Business Aircraft Association (NBAA) to talk about aircraft window safety. After every presentation, there was a question-and-answer session, during which I felt fulfilled by being able to educate people on window safety.

The AWR marketing and support team included, from left: Richard Mack, me, Ryan Cupery, Jennifer Cupery, and Lea Martin.

Me and my GTO alongside a Lockheed aircraft at Van Nuys Airport after a PAMA meeting.

Meeting Kathi

For 16 years, I was married to Clara Perez, who was from Argentina. We had two children, Jennifer and Ryan. Like many marriages, it ended, but we remained amicable.

On May 5, 1990, I was introduced to Kathi Gonzalez, from Redondo Beach, Calif., by a mutual friend during a Cinco de Mayo party at a tennis club. We started dating, and three years later, we were married.

Kathi and I on our wedding day.

Kathi and I seemed to have the same sense of humor, and we laughed a lot. Surprisingly, she was the president and owner of a staffing agency in Manhattan Beach, Calif. She had contracts with Northrop, Continental Airlines, and other aerospace firms to recruit and place engineers and administrative staff at those companies. She was adept at what she did, and kept her sense of humor so that when we went out, we would laugh a lot.

Kathi and I had similar backgrounds. We were both a fourth child, believed in God and liked to travel. I traveled with Northrop, working for CEO Thomas V. Jones, wherever the corporate jet excursions were going. I was their flight engineer, mechanic and steward. We always traveled first class.

Kathi was introduced to studying in Norway by a Norwegian college professor at El Camino College. She and two other classmates met the criteria to go by having a 3.0 grade point average and a minimum of sixty-two units. Before going overseas, they were required to study the Norwegian language in the language lab during summer school. However, when Kathi and her classmates arrived, they discovered almost everyone spoke English, or wanted to practice their English skills with them.

Upon arrival in Oslo, they checked into the dorms and immediately took a train downtown where all the American and other foreign students were invited to a reception hosted by King Olav V at the Royal Palace.

After the school year was completed, Kathi and two American classmates she had traveled with from the United States, toured sixteen countries that year while staying in student lodging at college dorms.

In 1992, I was skeptical in thinking Kathi would say "no" to my wedding proposal. I knew how much she loved her career, and it took a lot of time for her to coordinate and manage the company. However, much to my surprise, when I asked her to marry me, she said "yes." She had been working in human resources since 1976 and was ready for a change. So, it was the right time and right place for her to move forward.

In fact, Kathi's mother, Betty, thought she was working too much and bought her new suitcases for her birthday the year before as a hint that Kathi needed to go on vacation. Low and behold, Kathi agreed to sell her business, pack up, and move to Florida. It was a huge leap for her to leave her business, but also to become a stepmom to two teenagers.

Florida repair station

We rented a building in Port Charlotte, Fla., to set up a repair station. But, it wasn't long before we outgrew it and decided to purchase a larger facility. Because Kathi had sold her business, we had extra funds. It was a big help.

We bought a mini storage unit in North Port, Fla., and converted half of it into space for Aircraft Window Repairs, while the other half remained a storage unit. We hired A&Ps and were now set to do testing on coating for Dassault Falcon jets. That process took more than three years to complete.

After AWR successfully completed testing, the company received approval from the FAA and Dassault Falcon jets to apply our AWR8000 hard coating to lenses.

The AWR Florida inspection team included, from left: Me, Ryan Cupery, Herb Brock, and John Levy.

In Florida, we did a lot of window repair work in Tampa and Orlando in addition to AWR8000 lens hard coating. Due to inclement weather every summer, we decided to close the Florida facility. However, we accomplished our goal of testing for the hard coating business, and we received the FAA CC103 approval which still prevails today.

In 1994, we traveled back to California to visit the Getty Museum in Malibu where my ex-employer, Thomas V. Jones, the CEO of Northrop

Corporation, was receiving the Howard Hughes Memorial Award Trophy of Excellence from the California Aero Club. I felt both privileged and honored when Mrs. Jones called my name as Kathi and I entered the reception room. She said, "Tom, look who is here. It's Bob."

Part of my job, in addition to being chief mechanic, was to take Mrs. Jones shopping while Mr. Jones conducted business. I was quite flattered that she remembered me.

Char and Don Short (left) joined Kathi and I at the Getty Museum in Malibu, Calif. We were there to celebrate Thomas V. Jones, the former CEO of Northrop, being awarded the Howard Hughes Memorial Trophy of Excellence by the California Aero Club.

In 1995, Kathi and I purchased a home on a canal which led to the Gulf of Mexico. The home had a ten ton boat lift. Since we are both water lovers, we decided to purchase a boat and educate ourselves about navigating Florida waters.

Our boating proctor, Basil, suggested we buy a boat with a tunnel drive because the canals get very shallow, as little as two feet deep when the tide is out. I saw a 26-foot Penn Yan for sale, but it cost way too much money. Eventually, the price dropped and then went to view the boat.

To my surprise, it had a fly bridge, which was a bonus, especially when boating under the Florida sun. We couldn't wait to get in the water and head out for day-long excursions. We enjoyed visiting Don Pedro Island, which is a barrier island in Charlotte County in southwest Florida. We enjoyed swimming, snorkeling and collecting seashells.

Our 26-foot Penn Yan boat with a fly bridge.

It was great to enjoy an evening cruise or weekend outing after putting in hours of work with our great team at the Florida repair station. When we weren't boating, we enjoyed relaxing in our pool overlooking the canal.

Our backyard pool and Jacuzzi with Yorka, our pet floatie.
Our Penn Yan boat is on its boatlift in the background.

There is no question that being able to show a profit with this business is a very rewarding experience. We have been blessed and well-compensated for our quality service over the years. We live moderately and invest well, so during our down years, it also helped to be self-funded.

However, the biggest reward is that people from all over the country know about me and the business I started. We continue to get purchase orders from customers we served 40 years ago. That means the contacts I established during my Northrop years have been fulfilling.

In 1998, we were asked to attend a presentation in Nice, France, which was sponsored by the executives of Dassault Falcon Jet. Of the large number of clients from Europe and the United States, we were the only aircraft window repair company to be invited. We were honored to be able to shake hands with the president of Dassault Falcon Jet before a dinner party with approximately a hundred guests.

Here is a photo of me before giving a lecture at the Dassault Falcon Jet facility. The presentation was titled, "Corporate Jet Aircraft Window Care and Inspections."

After visiting Nice, we took a train to Cannes, France. Coincidentally, there was a film festival in town, and we were able to go sightseeing.

From there, we went to the French Riviera by train to view famous artist Pablo Picasso's beautiful home along the riviera. After that, we traveled to Tivoli Garden and Christiansborg Palace in Copenhagen, Denmark, where we spent three days before heading to Oslo, Norway.

In Oslo, we visited Vigeland Park, Munch Museum, the fjords, Holmenkollen Ski Museum, Frognerparken and the dorm where Kathi resided when she attended college.

Of course, during all the vacations and travel excursions we took time to communicate with the directors of maintenance at various airports to introduce them to Aircraft Window Repairs. To this day, our company still receives inquiries and purchase orders from many of the directors of maintenance we met in Europe.

Kathi and I enjoying lunch in Oslo, Norway.

Kathi and I in Tivoli Gardens in Copenhagen, Denmark.

We traveled another four weeks upon returning to the United States. We drove up to wine country in northern California, accompanied by Kathi's parents, Betty and Jess Gonzales. The four of us visited a winery owned by Kathi's aunt and uncle. We enjoyed VIP tours of neighboring wineries and even participated in a wine auction.

Being the businessman I am, I gave two winery owners information about Aircraft Window Repairs because they flew in corporate jets to the auction. We still receive purchase orders to repair their windows.

When my mother, Ruby, came to stay with us for the holidays, we took her boating. She loved spending time with us. My father, Rink, worked as a bank vice president for thirty years before he retired and bought a meat storage facility. Before passing away in the late 1970s, he also enjoyed helping my brother, Larry, with his farm on nights and weekends. I am an entrepreneur just like my father. I was sorry he couldn't enjoy our boating excursions and see my accomplishments. He would have been proud.

The Charles Taylor Award

The culmination of my career occurred in June 2015 when I received the FAA's coveted Charles Taylor Award. It recognizes the lifetime accomplishments of senior mechanics, and is presented to aircraft maintenance professionals for their skill, professionalism, and expertise as a "master mechanic." The FAA bestows no other awards that are more highly respected, greatly prized, or coveted than this master aviator award.

According to the award itself, it was presented in appreciation of my dedicated service, technical expertise, professionalism, and many outstanding maintenance contributions I made to further the cause of aviation safety. The certificate was signed by Michael Huerta, the FAA administrator. Needless to say, I was humbled beyond measure.

My old boss, Don Short, introduced me to the audience during the ceremony where I received the Charles Taylor Award.

The award was named in honor of Charles Taylor, the first mechanic in powered flight. He worked for Orville and Wilbur Wright, and is credited with building the engine for their first successful aircraft.

To be eligible to receive the award, I had to meet these requirements:

- Hold an FAA or U.S. Civil Aviation Authority (CAA) mechanic or repairman certificate.

- Have fifty or more years of civil or military maintenance experience, either performed consecutively or non-consecutively.

- Up to twenty of the required fifty years may be U.S. military experience; or in work as an uncertified person in a U.S. aviation maintenance facility that maintained U.S. registered aircraft, either domestic or overseas.

- Be a United States citizen.

- Not had any airman certificate revoked.

Millions of men and women have worked in the aviation maintenance industry since its inception in 1903, but only 3,239 people received the Charles Taylor Award, as of 2023. To be included in that esteemed group of aircraft maintenance professionals, was the pinnacle of my career. A banquet was held in my honor, and Kathi joined me in the celebration.

Chapter 9

Aircraft Window Repairs photos

Our building at 2207 Border Avenue in Torrance, Calif., from where we repaired aircraft windows and lenses for customers in the United States and Europe.

Hawker cabin windows.

Overhauled nav light lenses fit-checked on wingtips for proper fit.

Fighter windshield

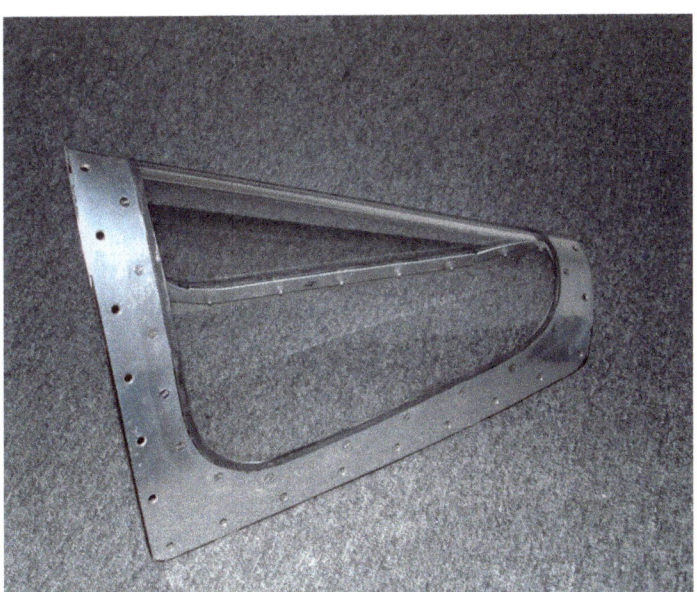

Hawker landing light lens.

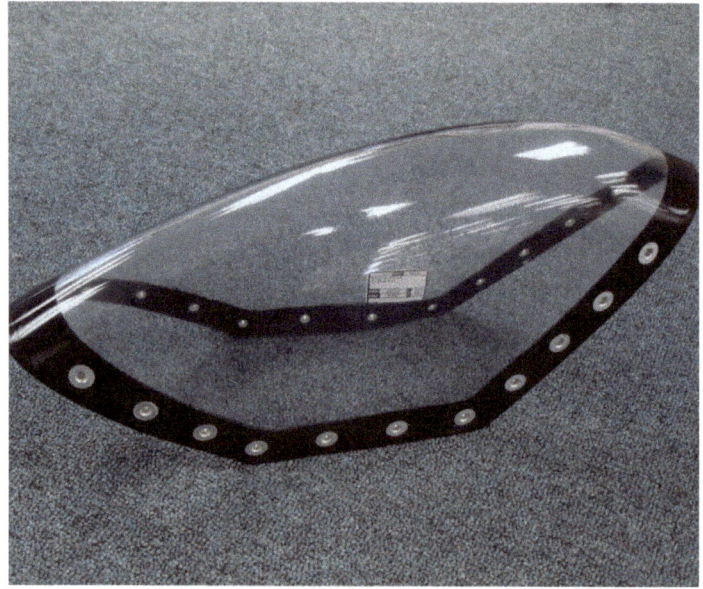

Nav light lens.

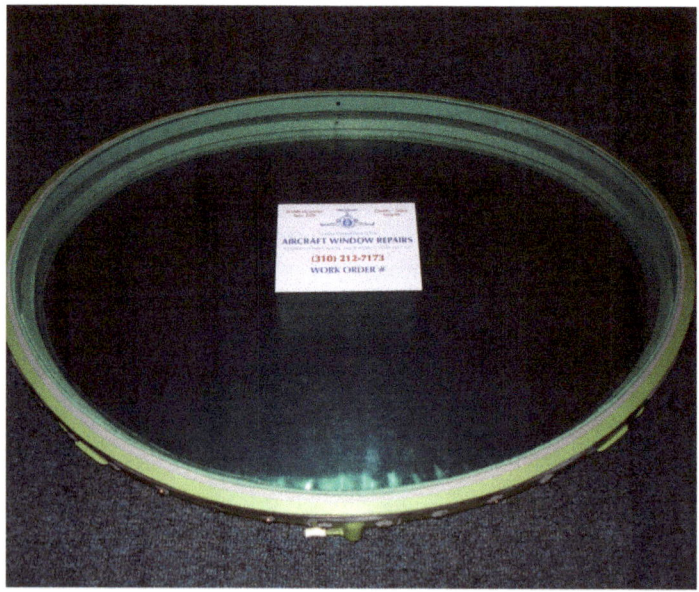

A completed aircraft window ready to ship back to a customer.

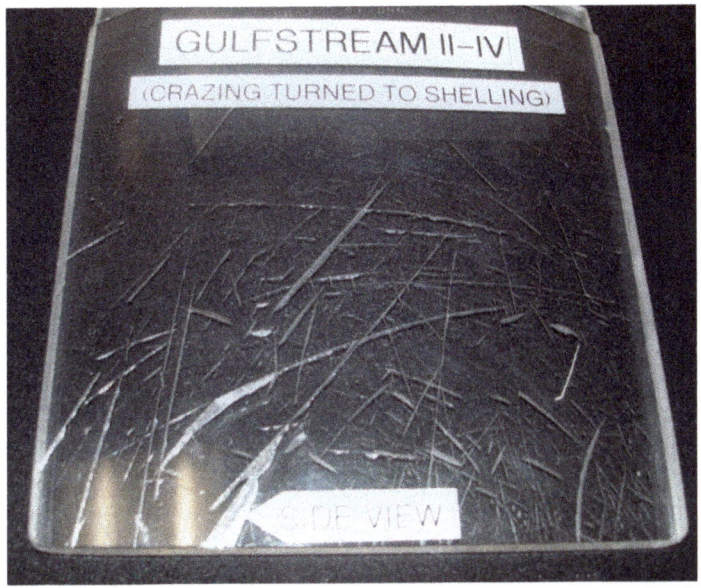

A window from a Gulfstream II-IV showing crazing which had turned to shelling.

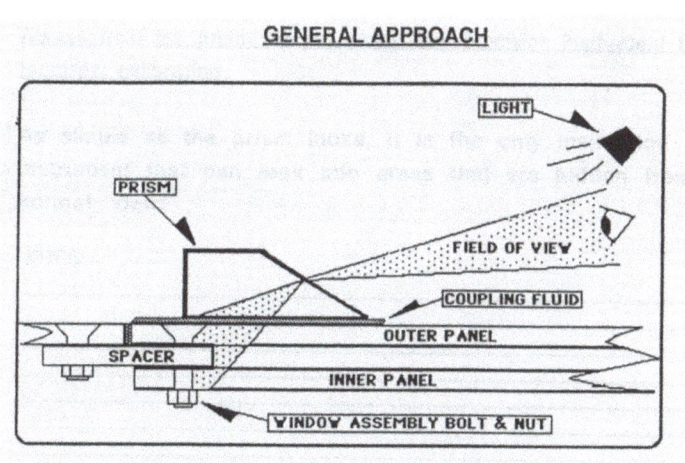

A surprising best-seller was our prism. Technicians could place the block edge next to an aircraft window and peer through the slanted edge to view under the frame to ensure the bolt and nut were firmly attached to the window assembly.

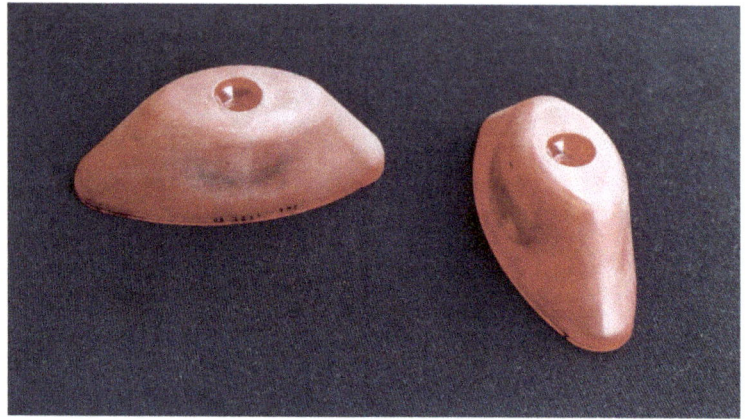

Navigation lights needing repair.

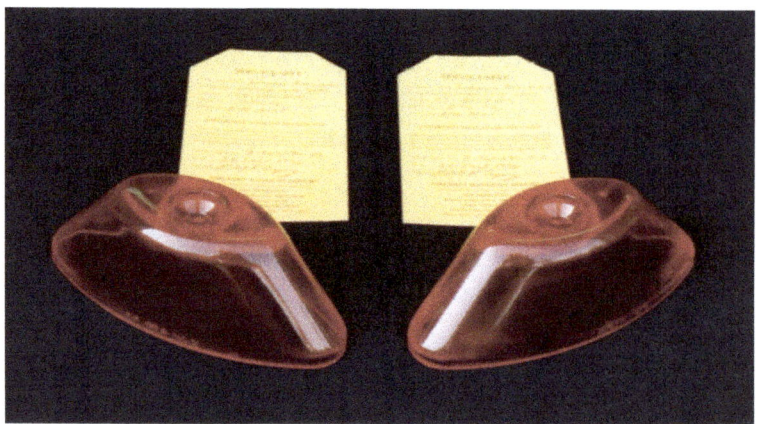

How the navigation lights appeared after the AWR crew worked its magic.

"2013" LENS RECEIVED (8 YEARS OLD) FOR POLISHING AND REHARDCOAT ***AVAILABLE TO EVERYONE***

THE ABOVE LENSE REPAIRED HARDCOATED AND RECERTIFIED DUAL RELEASE 8130-3 FAA/EASA

NOTE:
• CRAZING REMOVAL OF OUTER SURFACE ONLY
• NORMALLY 75% OF CRAZING IS REMOVED

This is a photo we used in marketing to show potential customers how the AWR team could transform an eight-year-old lens into a like-new hard-coated and recertified lens.

+ ✛ ✳ ✚ ✕ ▬▬▬▬▬▬▬▬▬▬▬▬▬▬▬▬▬▬▬

Monday, March 28, 2022

	Carriage Hall B			
GENERAL SESSION 1 8:00 – 9:05 a.m.	Welcome and Opening Remarks MnDOT Office of Aeronautics and Federal Aviation Administration Aircraft Maintenance Liability Update Greg Reigel Shackelford, Bowen, McKinley & Norton, LLP			
	Carriage Hall B	**Captain's Room**	**Harvest Room A**	**Harvest Room B/C**
BREAKOUT SESSION 2 9:10 – 10:00 a.m.	Borescopes: Beyond Basics See What You're Missing Zack Wessels ViewTech Borescopes	Marvel Schebler Carburetors Maintenance & Troubleshooting Alan Jesmer Tempest Air Group (Precision Airmotive)	Cylinder Review 2022 David Czarnecki Central Cylinder Service, Inc.	Fundamental Aircraft Heater Systems Tim Gauntt Hartzell Engine Technologies
BREAK (Carriage Hall A) 10:00 – 10:25 a.m.				
	Carriage Hall B	**Captain's Room**	**Harvest Room A**	**Harvest Room B/C**
BREAKOUT SESSION 3 10:30 – 11:20 a.m.	PT6 Maintenance Philosophy Keith Rash Covington Aircraft Engines	Wheel and Brake Maintenance Care Vern Rodgers Parker Cleveland Wheels and Brakes	Piston Engine Problems Dennis Wyman G&N Aircraft Inc.	RSA Fuel Injector Systems Maintenance & Troubleshooting Alan Jesmer Tempest Air Group (Precision Airmotive)
BREAKOUT SESSION 4 11:25 a.m. – 12:15 p.m.	Aircraft Maintenance From a Customer's Point of View Chris Meyer MnDOT Aeronautics	Engine Performance Monitoring Laboratory Services Ron Ashby Jet-Care International Inc.	Dynamic Propeller Balancing David Dykes ACES Systems	Fundamental Turbocharging Systems Tim Gauntt Hartzell Engine Technologies
LUNCH (Garden City Ballroom) 12:15 – 1:30 p.m.				
BREAKOUT SESSION 5 1:30 – 2:20 p.m.	Aircraft Window Inspection and Maintenance Robert R Cupery Aircraft Window Repairs	Installed Engine Performance Monitoring Ron Ashby Jet-Care International Inc.	Lead Acid Aircraft Battery Airworthiness Mike Abrams Concorde Battery Corporation	Workplace Human Factors and Distractions Tim Gauntt Hartzell Engine Technologies
GENERAL SESSION 6 2:25 – 3:15 p.m.	What would you do in these Maintenance Situations? Mike Millard FAA, Air Safety Inspector, AFS-830			
BREAK (Carriage Hall A) 3:15 – 3:45 p.m.				
BREAKOUT SESSION 7 3:45 – 4:35 p.m.	Engine Failure after Maintenance Troy Srekas FAASTeam Program Manager, Airworthiness, Minneapolis FSDO	Required Special Session for All AMT College Students	Removal, Installation, Care and Storage of Pneumatic Deicers Steve Mayer SMR Technologies, Ice Shield Deicing Systems	Who Needs A&P's When You Have YouTube Videos? Tim Gauntt Hartzell Engine Technologies

I was honored to be a guest speaker at the 2022 Minnesota Technician and IA Renewal Conference March 28 and 29 at the Earle Brown Heritage Center in Brooklyn Center. Sponsored by the Minnesota Department of Transportation, I was asked to speak about inspecting and maintaining aircraft windows.

Chapter 10

Epilogue

It has been a fun journey, and not at all like work for me. That's why I am still going into the facility for a few hours every day just to see what's going on, and to help when needed. My staff doesn't really need any supervision because they're all professionals. However, every once in a while, they encounter a challenge that I can help them resolve, and that's very rewarding for me.

Now that I am in my late seventies, people often ask me when I am going to sell my business and retire. But, why should I? I am still having fun and still making an impact on my business. I truly don't know what I would do if I were to completely retire. I certainly don't want to become a couch potato and watch television until I die.

My friends and family often ask why I don't retire, relax, and travel. Our accountant asks the same thing because, apparently, we have a lot of assets and real estate. But, it's not about the money and it never has been. It is about the process of helping, giving, and participating.

I feel extremely proud that so many companies have jumped in and tried to copy Aircraft Window Repairs (AWR). A lot of them do it for the money, which is never a good idea. You either like the business, or you don't. If there was an Academy Award for quality aircraft repair, I am sure AWR would win the top prize. But, that's only in Hollywood.

Today, I'm technically a "senior citizen," even though I don't look or feel my age, according to our family, friends, and even our primary doctor. During 2020, before the COVID vaccine was released, we decided to eat less and move more. We watched all of our important numbers, such as body mass index, cholesterol, and triglycerides. We ate at home for a year, walked, and swam a lot. As a result, I lost thirty-five pounds and Kathi lost ten pounds. She wondered how we gained so much weight over the years and did not feel uncomfortable.

As for travel, we like to visit our relatives. But, when it comes to world travel, I have already traveled first class with Northrop, so you could say I am spoiled. Kathi has been to 16 countries in Europe.

On the personal side, Kathi and I live very fiscally-conservative lives. It helps that both of us are members of the baby boomer generation. It also helped tremendously that we were investing our money, rather than spending it, back in the 1970s and 1980s.

In 2002, when developing a succession plan, AWR's financial advisor suggested that Kathi and I step back and allow management to take over. But, we enjoy planning and seeing a project to completion. You could actually say it is "fun," and changing technology certainly makes it easier to remain in business than it did twenty years ago.

Because I'm still having fun and continue to make an impact on the aircraft transparency market, you might say it is in my blood. I discovered a purpose for my life and, with God's guidance, I intend to pursue it as long as I have air in my lungs.

I also need to acknowledge the tremendous contributions my children, Ryan and Jennifer, have made to my life over the years. When they were young, I wanted to be a big part of their lives. That's why I gave up flying around the globe so I could shuttle my children to various activities near our home. Ryan worked for AWR in California and Florida. He is an excellent technician and certified FAA inspector. Today, Ryan lives in Redondo Beach, Calif., where he works as a handyman for his own company, RECreation.

Jennifer currently owns a hobby ranch in northwest Florida with her husband of 30 years. A graduate of the University of California in Irvine, she is a master gardener herself who is actively involved in helping others to fall in love with gardening. She has served as the president and district director of her garden club, and served as a judge at various flower shows in Florida. Jennifer also loves butterflies. She has served as president of the Panhandle Butterfly House and Nature Center in Milton, Fla., and as president of Butterflies in Motion, Inc.

As children, Ryan and Jennifer learned to drive by navigating a go-kart along the alley behind our first repair station in Torrance, Calif. They did a fine job and eventually learned to drive my GTO as teenagers. I could not be more proud of both of them.

No regrets in life

In this learning curve of life, I feel very blessed to say I have no regrets.

When we opened the Florida Aircraft Window Repairs location in 1993, Kathi and I actually moved to Florida. It was a great learning experience, and no one ever stops learning. We were frequently flying back to California for meetings at the Torrance Repair Station, and those visits gave Kathi a chance to visit her parents, family, and friends.

Kathi had a background in human resources for seventeen years before joining Aircraft Window Repairs. She owned a staffing business, so she had no problem adjusting to a different profession with a lot less stress. Managing human resources can be challenging work, and Kathi was ready for a change in her daily life.

It was almost like God had a plan and we followed it. We are both the fourth child in our families, so maybe that had something to do with our work ethic as well. Neither of us is afraid of a business challenge.

I found my purpose

Sometimes, it is hard to see the impact little life changes can have over the course of an entire lifetime. That was certainly true for me. Just think:

- If a band director had not needed a tuba player when I was in high school, then I never would have taken my first flight on his two-seater, single-engine aircraft. That experience sparked my interest in an aviation career.

- If I had not injured myself playing football, then I would have joined the U.S. Marine Corps rather than the U.S. Air Force. That experience taught me to be an aircraft mechanic.

- If I had not been placed in an aviation maintenance specialty while in the military, then I never would have had an opportunity to lead a team, and transform a dysfunctional ground equipment station into a stellar operation.

- That position in the military opened the door for me to get a job with Northrop as a flight engineer on the company's private jet.

- That experience required me to travel extensively, and develop relationships with the directors of maintenance at airports around the world. I flew four million miles to visit thirty-five countries.

- On one of those trips, I had a chance conversation with a Northrop executive and simply mentioned that I desired to be closer to home and my growing family. A short-time later, that executive opened a door for me to get a job in product support as a service engineer working on the company's F5 aircraft.

- That opportunity kept me in Los Angeles full time.

- Through that job, I developed a reputation for providing outstanding customer service to Northrop clients. I helped develop solutions to so many tricky problems that I became known as the "engine man."

- That experience opened a door to become the manager of international quality assurance, which reconnected me to airports around the globe without having to travel so much.

- That position opened my eyes to a problem that plagued all private jet owners in that their windows had to be frequently replaced, which was very expensive. As an experiment, I got permission to try refurbishing windows on my own. The company loved the quality of my work, and the fact I could repair a window for a fraction of the price of replacing it.

- That realization sparked an idea to refurbish windows as a side business by working out of my garage.

- The quality-assurance job also gave me a lot of flexibility to meet with customers to give them an estimate to fix their windows at night and on weekends.

- Business grew so quickly that I had to leave my job to manage my own company. That experience provided me with an income and a lifestyle I never dreamed was possible.

Many firsts

Over the course of my life, I have been fortunate to be a part of many "firsts," including:

- My uncle, Martin, discovered a new use for Teflon while at Dupont where he created a tape that could be used on threaded surfaces. It was called Tape Seal.

- My father was the first person to manufacture that Teflon tape, and he shipped it all over the world.

- I served on the flight crew of the first Gulfstream II aircraft to be certified by the FAA as an air taxi.

- My company, Aircraft Window Repairs, was the first firm to receive FAA certification for aircraft window repairs.

Conclusion

Yes, the Lord has been very good to me over the years. I have repeatedly asked for his help and his guidance. I did so not just when it could provide me material success, but to give me knowledge and wisdom to make the right decisions, and to do whatever He wanted me to do.

Of course, I made my own share of mistakes either by not consulting with God, or by ignoring his instructions and going my own way. There were several critical points in my life where the course I followed may not always have been my own choosing.

Being unable to enter the U.S. Marine Corps would be one example. While it may have seemed tragic at the time, ultimately, the path I was put on turned out to be the right course, not just for my benefit, but for the benefit of many others.

I urge people of all ages to place their reliance on God's divine wisdom and his limitless spiritual and physical resources. I'd like to share a prayer I have recited often:

Thank you, dear Lord, for letting me be born in America with a great heritage of freedom; and for letting me grow up in a small town in Wisconsin, which was part of the grass roots of America where I received a solid foundation upon which to build my life.

Thank you for my God-fearing parents who taught me the real value of following your way, which shaped my understanding; and for the support of a loyal family who have consistently supported me and encouraged me along my journey.

Thank you, Lord, for all the opportunities in this life that you have revealed to me, and for the faith to trust you in pursuing them, even when I did not see a benefit. Thank you for all my personal, occupational, financial, and spiritual blessings. Amen.

THE END

Chapter 11

Photos throughout the years

Me and my 1964 Pontiac tri-powered GTO convertible in front of an F-111 jet in 2015.

Kathi and I took part in the U.S. Department of Transportation conference where I made a presentation on inspection authorization renewals on March 28, 2022. The event took place in Brooklyn Center, Minn.

It was a productive day of fishing off the coast of Florida in the Gulf of Mexico.

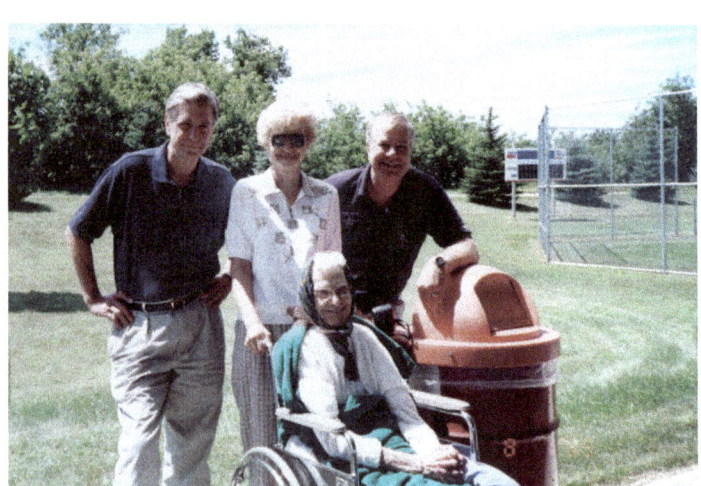

Stan, LaVerne and I with our mother, Ruby, during a day at the park in Friesland, Wis., around 2000.

Ruby and Rink Cupery, circa 1973.

Our home in Florida with our backyard and dock where we experienced many fishing trips with me as captain of my Penn Yan boat.

This photo was taken when I was on the fly bridge of our Penn Yan boat serving as captain near Don Pedro Island, a barrier island in southwest Florida. My mother, Ruby, left, had accidentally cut her hand on a fish hook and Kathi was ensuring Ruby kept ice on her hand.

Jennifer and Ryan having breakfast on Veterans Day 2019.

*Ryan Cupery with a fighter jet canopy at the Aircraft
Window Repair station.*

My daughter, Jennifer Cupery Weber, giving a lecture at the Milton Garden Club in Florida.

Farmers & Merchants Union Bank in Friesland, Wis., where my father, Rink Cupery, served as bank president for 30 years.

My grandfather, Ely Cupery, left, and my father, Rink Cupery, served on the Friesland Chamber of Commerce.

My father, Rink Cupery, at a trade show in 1959 in
Birmingham, Ala.

Gathered for Sunday dinner, my family included, from left, my brother, Larry; sister, Laverne; brother, Stan; father; Rink; me; and my mother, Ruby.

Kathi with her father, Jess Gonzalez, when her parents came to Florida to preview our new business. Kathi's mother, Betty, took this photo.

The Charlotte Sun newspaper in Charlotte County, Fla.,
welcomed Aircraft Window Repairs with a full-page article
about our business.

Kathi and I at our storage facility in Northport, Fla.

My mother, Ruby Cupery, and I outside of our storage facility in Northport, Fla. Many days, she would come in to watch me manage Aircraft Window Repairs, which occupied half of the buildings.

Kathi and I at the Liberty Bell in Philadelphia, Penn. In the summer of 2002, we took a three-month driving trip to visit the Catskill Mountains in New York. Along the way, we visited customers in Chicago, Niagara Falls, Buffalo, Rochester, Syracuse and Albany.

On a trip to northern California, we toured the Storybook Mountain Vineyards in Calistoga, Calif., at the top of Napa Valley. On the left, I'm with Kathi's parents, Betty and Jess Gonzalez. On the right, Kathi is with our relatives, Bill and Patsy Roddis.

My father-in-law, Jess Gonzalez, right, and I attended a wine auction at the Roddis Celler.

Me giving a VIP tour to my grandnephew, Joseph Pressler, Jr., who is sitting in the cockpit of an F5 aircraft at the Western Museum of Flight in Torrance, Calif., in November 2022.

*Kathi surprised me around 2005 by having
a bookmark made for me as part of a
fundraiser to support the armed forces.*

Chapter 12

Celebrities I have flown

In addition to the luminaries we shuttled around the world when I was the flight engineer on the Gulfstream II-IV, our crew flew also shuttled many celebrities of film, music and television, including:

Alley, Kirstie

Alpert, Herb and the Tijuana Brass

Anka, Paul

Avnet, Jon

Ball, Lucille

Bates, Kathy

Bergen, Edgar

Black, Clint

Bono, Sony and Cher

Burton, Richard

Callas, Charles

Candy, John

Cantinflas

Capshaw, Kate

Carrey, Jim

Cassidy, Shaun

Channing, Carol

"Chicago"

Claman, Liz

Coppola, Francis Ford

Cosby, Bill

Cruise, Tom

Davis, Jr., Sammy

De Niro, Robert

Dennis, Day

Devine, Andy

DeVito, Danny

Douglas, Kirk

Dunne, Irene

Ferrare, Cristina

Fiennes, Ray

Fox, Michael J.

Frey, Glenn

Furness, Betty

Gavin, John

Geffen, David

Gill, Vince

Granville, Bonita

Hanks, Tom

Hope, Bob

Howard, Ron

Hunter, Holly

Katzenberg, Jeffrey

Kidman, Nicole

Kingsley, Ben

Lansbury, Angela

Laurie, Piper

Linkletter, Art

Lloyd, Christopher

Martin, Dick

Martin, Steve

Meadows, Audrey

Molen, Gerald

Murphy, Eddie

Murphy, George

Nelson, Craig T.

O'Brien, Hugh

O'Connor, Donald

Pacino, Al

Paxton, Bill

Peck, Gregory

Perlman, Rhea

Pleshette, Suzanne

Presley, Elvis

Preston, Kelly

Reagan, Ron

Reitman, Ivan

Robbins, Tim

Rowan, Dan

Russell, Kurt

Sarandon, Susan

Schwarzenegger, Arnold

Scorsese, Martin

Short, Martin

Shriver, Maria

Sinatra, Frank

Sinise, Gary

Spielberg, Steven

St. John, Jill

Stallone, Sylvester

Stewart, Jimmy

Stewart, Rod

Stone, Sharon

Streep, Meryl

Taylor, Elizabeth

"The Faces"

Travolta, John

Vaughn, Vince

Wagner, Robert

Wasserman, Lewis

Williams, Robin

Wilson, Rita

Wolf, Tom

Zemekis, Robert

Source: Don Short, the pilot who kept air logs of places we visited and passengers we transported.

Chapter 13

Awards and honors

It was an absolute honor to receive the Charles Taylor Award, which is the highest award a maintenance professional can receive from the Federal Aviation Administration.

 **Federal Aviation Administration**

2015
Charles E. Taylor
Master Mechanic Award
(CETMMA)

Presented to:
Robert R. Cupery

Cupery Corporation
d/b/a Aircraft Window Repairs Est.1979

A flyer announcing the award banquet.

CETMMA is for lifetime accomplishments of senior mechanics
The award named for Charles E. Taylor the first aviation powered flight
where he served as the Wright Brothers mechanic and is
credited with designing & building the engine for their
first successful aircraft.

Many thanks to my beloved spouse Kathi
& The AWR Team
Shawn, Armondo, Lea, Toni, Lauren, Ron, Juan,
Danny, Meechie, Richard, Vangie, Frank,
Natalie, Susan, Roberta, Sean & other
previous AWR Team Members

*This was placed at everyone's seat during the banquet when I received
the Charles E. Taylor Award.*

Chapter 14

Letters of appreciation

The following pages show copies of letters of appreciation I have received over the years. They start in my high school years, continue through my time in the U.S. Air Force, and conclude with letters I received during my flying days.

T H E   U N I V E R S I T Y   O F   W I S C O N S I N
EXTENSION MUSIC DEPARTMENT

548 State Street   Madison 6, Wisconsin

Mr. Robert R. Cupery — Bass
Route 2
Cambria, Wisconsin

Dear Robert:

We are very happy to inform you that you have been selected to participate
in the 1961 State 4-H Band and its activities in the 1961 State 4-H Club
Week in Madison, June 13-16, and the Wisconsin State Fair in Milwaukee,
August 14-17.

Please fill out, sign and mail the enclosed postal card, stating if you
will be able to participate. The deadline date on which all these cards
must be in is May 15. No exceptions can be made to this date. Mail it
immediately!

The instrument to which you are assigned is indicated after your name,
and is based upon your application blank. In a few cases, instruments
can be furnished if you cannot bring one. However, make every effort
to bring your own instrument, since you will no doubt perform better
on your own instrument. Indicate very carefully on the return postal
card if you will be bringing the instrument indicated after your name,
or if you will need the indicated instrument furnished. If you need
an instrument furnished, list the exact type - such as Eb bass or BBb
bass. Music will not be sent in advance to members of the State 4-H
Band, as is being done with the State 4-H Chorus.

Your first obligation to the State 4-H Band will be on Tuesday, June 13,
at 11:00 A.M., in Music Hall Auditorium. Bring your instrument to this
rehearsal on Tuesday and also bring a folding music rack. Cornet,
trumpet and trombone players, bring your mutes.

The dress for the concert which the State 4-H Band and Chorus will give
on Thursday evening during State 4-H Club Week is herein described:
Girls will wear simple white dresses of street length with brown or
black shoes. Boys will wear white trousers, white long-sleeved shirts,
official 4-H green neckties (which can be purchased during State 4-H
Club Week for $.90) and brown or black shoes. All band members will
also wear the National 4-H Jacket, which may be purchased during State
4-H Club Week at a special reduced rate of $4.60 each. If you already
own a 4-H Jacket or can borrow one, please indicate this on your reply;
it will help us in ordering a supply to have on hand during State Club
Week.

*A letter announcing my acceptance into the Wisconsin 4-H Band the
summer of 1961.*

State 4-H Band - page 2

All arrangements for your being at State 4-H Club Week (transportation, housing, registration, payment of fees, etc.) will be handled by your County Extension Agent.

These are the opportunities for members of the 1961 State 4-H Band.

State 4-H Club Week - June 13-16, 1961

During State 4-H Club Week the 1961 State Band will organize and rehearse intensively. At the end of Club Week the Band, with the State 4-H Chorus, will present a thrilling musical production in the Union Theatre.

State Fair - August 14-17, 1961

During State Fair the State 4-H Band and Chorus will present the musical production learned during Club Week at various times during the day for three days. Costs for lodging and meals and transportation will be provided for each member of the Band and Chorus for this event by the State Fair. When you are in the State 4-H Band it will be impossible for you to represent your county in the 1961 dress review or demonstration program at the State Fair.

I'm sure you realize the importance of the same personnel participating in all of the above events. We shall expect you to fulfill your obligations in each of these events; excuses will be made only in cases of extreme necessity.

The U.W. Extension Music Department is extremely happy to be cooperating with the U.W. College of Agriculture and the State 4-H Program in working with 4-H people in music throughout Wisconsin. We certainly are looking forward to working with you in the 1961 State 4-H Band. The State Band and Chorus are going to be two outstanding organizations. During Club Week we will be expecting you to attend and take part in the other sessions of the State 4-H Club Week as well as the rehearsal sessions. If you have any questions, please feel free to write me.

Sincerely yours,

William L. Johnston
Assistant Professor of Music
Extension Music Department

WLJ:fh
Encl.

445th Fighter Interceptor Squadron (ADC)
UNITED STATES AIR FORCE
Wurtsmith Air Force Base, Michigan

REPLY TO
ATTN OF: 445 MSq-OM   15 March 1965

SUBJECT: Airman of the Month

TO: CCR

1. Airman second class Robert R. Cupery, AF 16749296, has been assigned to the periodic dock section of Organizational Maintenance from December 64 to the present. During this time he has shown outstanding initiative and drive. His ability on the job and his devotion to duty have been an example and guide to younger airmen assigned from Technical School. His extensive knowledge of the F-101 aircraft and his technical ability have been proven many times by the extremely low number of discrepancies he generates.

2. Airman Cupery is one of the most intelligent and resourceful people I have encountered. He is quick to grasp the concepts of a new situation and can perform the duties assigned to him in a most exemplary manner.

3. The military bearing and dress of Airman Cupery are above reproach. His conduct and appearance set an example of the highest caliber at all times. He is definitely a career-motivated airman and has proven himself to be a great value to the Air Force.

4. With these qualifications, I wholeheartedly recommend Airman Cupery for Airman of the Month for February 1965.

Norman L. Bush
SSgt, USAF
Periodic Dock Chief

My recommendation to be honored as Airman of the Month.

Memorandum
Northrop Corporation

In reply refer to: **8868-80-110**
JMF:him

To: Whom It May Concern   From: Service Engineering

Subject: LETTER OF RECOMMENDATION – MR. ROBERT CUPERY   Date: 15 July 1980

Copies: File   Ref:

Mr. Robert Cupery came to work as a Service Engineer late in 1976 after several years of outstanding service as a crew member on Northrop Corporate Transport aircraft. He was assigned responsibility for investigation of F-5 field problems reported by customers or Northrop Technical Representatives on the engines, engine instruments, fire warning, landing gear, nose wheel steering, landing gear electrical systems and associated support equipment. Investigative responsibility included screening of incoming reports, determining if a exhibit would be required, arranging for delivery of an exhibit, coordinating investigative activities involving Engineering, Quality Control, Vendors and Integrated Logistics Support, and preparation of the final Northrop report to the customer. Following submission of investigation reports, Mr. Cupery was responsible for monitoring follow up actions such Technical Order changes, or publishing interim technical data and providing it to field users pending distribution of formal data.

Mr. Cupery did his assigned tasks with zeal, dedication and energy. He was particularly effective in evaluation of problems to determine the need for immediate field action and in evaluating recommended solutions as to suitability for the field environment. During Mr. Cupery's assignment to Service Engineering he completed an off-duty education program and earned a degree in Business Administration. His studies resulted in a rapid growth in writing ability and understanding of administrative matters.

I highly recommend that Mr. Cupery eventually be returned to a Technical assignment. His initiative, management ability, and technical comprehension make him an ideal candidate for increased responsibility in a technical supervisory position.

J. M. Foley, Manager
Service Engineering
Orgn. 8868/AR, Ext. 6350

NORTHROP

From J.M. Foley, the manager of service engineering at Northrop.

DART
INDUSTRIES INC.

JUSTIN DART
PRESIDENT

April 12, 1973

Dear Bob:

There is no way we can express our gratitude and
thanks to you for such a marvelous trip in the G-2.
The entire trip couldn't have been smoother or better
handled -- despite the two cracked windshields. I
am afraid you have spoiled us for any future jaunts
of this type.

Mrs. Dart and all the others who were aboard join
me in sending our grateful thanks,

Justin

Mr. Bob Cupery
Northrop Corporation
1800 Century Park East
Century City
Los Angeles, California 900

JUSTIN DART

Many thanks!

PRESIDENT
DART INDUSTRIES INC.   LOS ANGELES

P. O. BOX 3157 TERMINAL ANNEX LOS ANGELES CALIFORNIA 90051

From Justin Dart, the president of Dart Industries.

Georgia Aviation Hall of Fame

Joseph C. Miles

"Korean War Veteran, Northrop University Director Emeritus"

(1924 - 2015

12/22/15

Bob Cupery
c/o Aircraft Window Repairs
2207 Border Ave
Torrance, CA 90501

Dear Bob,

Thank you for the Christmas card and the DVD of your award presentation. That was quite an honor you received. I am sure that Joe would have loved to see the DVD, or even better to have been able to attend in person.

I am sorry to have to tell you that Joe died on July 13 of this year. His health had been in decline for several months. Finally, he went into the hospital and didn't come out. The doctors say his death was caused by general organ failure.

We miss Joe very much. Pearl has now moved to a Personal Care Facility in Harlem, GA. I will see that she gets your Christmas card. If you would like to contact her directly, her new address follows:

Pearl P. Miles
c/o West Forrest Personal Care Home
280 West Forrest Street
Harlem, GA 30814
Telephone: 706-556-6005

Best wishes,

Ron Miles

Ron

P-51 MUSTANG PILOTS ASSOCIATION
Joseph C. Miles
Director Emeritus - Institute of Technology
Northrop-Rice

Georgia Aviation Hall of Fame - 2007

442 Aumond Road, Augusta, Georgia 30909   (706) 733-8376

AUGUSTUS F. HAWKINS
21ST DISTRICT, CALIFORNIA

COMMITTEE:
EDUCATION AND LABOR

1124 HOUSE OFFICE BUILDING
WASHINGTON, D.C.

MRS. JUANITA BARBEE
ADMINISTRATIVE ASSISTANT

LOS ANGELES OFFICE:
8563 SOUTH BROADWAY
TELEPHONE: 750-0260

CHARLES E. KNOX
SPECIAL ASSISTANT

Congress of the United States
House of Representatives
Washington, D.C. 20515

July 1, 1971

Mr. Bob Cupery, Flight Engineer
Northrup Corporation
1800 Century Park East
Century City, California 90067

Dear Mr. Cupery:

On behalf of Congressman Hawkins and the staff, I extend
appreciation for your efficient and courteous service
on our recent flight to Washington, D.C.

Both you and the other members of the crew made our trip
comfortable and an experience long to be remembered.

Sincerely yours,

Charles E. Knox
Special Assistant to

AUGUSTUS F. HAWKINS
Member of Congress

CEK:dc
cc: Tom Jones

From Congressman Augustus Hawkins

February 11, 1972

Thank you, Bob . . .

Just want you to know how much
I appreciate that wonderful flight
home from Colorado.

Gratefully,

Lucy

Lucy

From Lucille Ball

Chapter 15

Publications

Over the years, I have been fortunate to be the subject of several magazine articles. My favorite articles are shown on the following pages.

I was honored to be the cover story for Director of Maintenance magazine after receiving the Charles E. Taylor Award

DEC 2017
JAN 2018

20

50
Micro-management constricts
the working environment
and productivity.

24

6

Photos by LeMar Photography & Video

contents

FEATURES

Photos by LaMar Photography & Video

ROBERT CUPERY

ROBERT CUPERY'S CAREER IN AVIATION IS AS VARIED AS IT GETS, CULMINATING AS THE RECIPIENT OF THE 2015 CHARLES E. TAYLOR MASTER MECHANIC AWARD.

The 73-year-old from Palos Verde, CA, got his first taste of aviation as a 17-year-old high school student playing in a marching band. He played tuba for his own high school in Cambria, WI, when he was approached by the owner of a local canning company who offered to give Cupery flying lessons if he would also march in the band in nearby Pardeeville.

"The school needed a tuba player, so I marched in that band, too, and the man was true to his word. He gave me some flying lessons until my mother found out about it and put an end to my flying career," Cupery explains. "Watching airplanes was amazing, but

flying one took my interest in aviation to a whole new level."

After graduating from high school in 1962, he followed his brother's footsteps by joining the U.S. Air Force, volunteering in hopes for an opportunity to "see the world." But, after completing his initial training, Cupery was stationed at Wurtsmith Air Force Base in Oscada, MI, which he described as being further north and even colder than Wisconsin.

In the military, Cupery trained to repair F-100 aircraft and spent his entire four-year enlistment servicing F-101 aircraft, which patrolled the North American Distant Early Warning (DEW) line along

the Canadian border during the Vietnam War. It was a relatively bland experience since his base only went on alert twice, once when the Soviet Union placed missiles in Cuba and again when President Kennedy was assassinated.

However, he excelled at his job and, as an airman first class, he was selected to lead a team of technicians to maintain the squadron commander's jet. Although his commander enticed him to re-enlist by offering a fourth stripe, Cupery opted to leave at the end of his enlistment, just three months before the unit shipped out to Vietnam.

After separating from the military, Cupery vetoed the idea of working on his brother's farm and instead decided to continue his training as an aircraft mechanic by attending one of nation's elite aviation technical schools.

"I spoke with the base's McDonald-Douglas rep and he recommended three schools: Spartan, Embry-Riddle and Northrop Institute," he explains. "I picked Northrop because it was based in southern California."

So, when he was 22, he moved to California and joined a class of 55 students, of which only 12 graduated. Cupery was third in his class despite working his way through school as a bartender for Shakey's Pizza and a bouncer for Mother's Tavern where he'd trade his nightly free pizza for beer.

After graduating, he decided he missed the changing seasons and moved to Minneapolis to work for Northwest Orient servicing Electra aircraft as well as 707 and 727 commercial jets.

"Then, the first winter came and I remembered why I left Michigan in the first place," Cupery explains. "I came out of the hangar one night and couldn't find my car because it was buried in snow. I complained to my father and he told me the best time to move was when I could fit everything I owned in the trunk of my car."

AN OPEN DOOR

So, he packed his belongings and returned to southern California where he worked as an inspector/mechanic for Rajay Turbochargers in Long Beach. However, he only worked there a few weeks before a Northrop representative called out of the blue to ask him to become a flight engineer for a new Gulfstream II private jet.

He interviewed with the president of the company and with Don Short, a pilot who flew Air Force One for President Lyndon Johnson. When he returned to work the next day, he learned that Northrop had already called his boss, who handed him a paycheck for the entire week and directed him to report to Northrop the next day.

Cupery processed into Northrop that Friday, received another paycheck and a ticket to Savannah, GA, to watch the new Gulfstream jet being built.

"We had serial number 42 and it was the first Gulfstream to ever receive an FAA 135.2 air taxi certificate," he explains, noting that he put 4 million air miles on that jet in just a few years.

To get ready to work as a flight engineer, Cupery had to leave Savannah for Canada to learn about the Rolls-Royce Spey engine that powered the GII jet. From there, he flew to Pittsburg to work as a personal steward aboard a private jet owned by U.S. Steel Corporation. For two weeks he learned the ins and outs of catering to dignitaries.

Next, he returned to California to learn about the GII's navigation system for a few weeks before making a quick jaunt to Phoenix for training on auxiliary power units. When all his training was complete, so was the aircraft and he returned to Los Angeles just in time for flight testing.

As a flight engineer, it was Cupery's job to assist the cockpit crew during takeoff and landing. Then, once in the air, he became the cabin steward ensuring that passengers had plenty to eat and drink during the flight. After landing, he transformed into a mechanic to inspect the aircraft and facilitate any needed repairs.

"I fixed that plane everywhere in the world," he explains. "I once had to replace two windshields in a rainstorm while visiting Rio de Janeiro. I had to work 40 hours straight to keep everyone on schedule."

In that instance, the plane had been rented by Justin Dart, the CEO of Kraft, Inc. He was so grateful for Cupery's effort to maintain the schedule that he invited the mechanic to join the staff on a river cruise along the Amazon at the next stop. Despite having worked nearly two days without rest, Cupery jumped at the opportunity.

However, while navigating down the piranha-infested waters, the

boat's engine broke down. After a short delay, Dart recommended that Cupery go below to assist the ship's crew in diagnosing the problem. Within a few minutes of entering the engine room, which he describes as a fire hazard with grease and oil all over the place, the engine fired up. When he emerged from the engine room, Cupery got a standing ovation despite never having picked up a wrench.

"I graciously accepted the applause," he says.

SHUTTLING CELEBRITIES

Northrop used the GII aircraft to visit all 35 nations that acquired an F-5 fighter. They flew to air bases in the Atlantic region in June 1969 and the Pacific in November of that year — around the world in each direction. When corporate executives weren't using the jet for business, the company rented it out to other people.

So, in 1972, Cupery began what he describes as the most memorable period of his career — shuttling celebrities around the globe. It was

a tough economic time for America and Northrop wanted to show prospective buyers that the GII could be rented out as a taxi to help offset the cost of ownership.

"Everyone wanted to rent the plane because we were the first one to use a Gulfstream jet," he explains. "Before that, Learjets were popular private air taxis. It was funny because at many places we visited people kept asking if it was a Learjet."

The first paying customer was Howard Hughes, who needed to be picked up following an earthquake in Nicaragua and shuttled to Canada. Cupery also shuttled several World War II fighter aces on a trip to the Orient, including Johnny Alison, David Lee "Tex" Hill, and Arnie Blunt.

He even flew the Shaw of Iran, which was an interesting experience requiring additional training in protocol to learn not to touch the dignitary. An aide would take the Shaw's coat and pass it to Cupery.

Other well-known clients included Sonny and Cher, and the "Rat Pack"

...his most famous passenger was likely Elvis Presley, with whom Cupery spent his 27th birthday singing gospel songs with the legendary entertainer in his Las Vegas Hilton hotel suite.

of Dean Martin, Frank Sinatra, Peter Lawford, Joey Bishop and Sammy Davis, Jr. However, his most famous passenger was likely Elvis Presley, with whom Cupery spent his 27th birthday singing gospel songs with the legendary entertainer in his Las Vegas Hilton hotel suite. The crew shuttled Presley to events so often that the plane was featured several times in the documentary movie Elvis on Tour.

"Elvis was a genuinely nice man and very interesting to talk with," says Cupery. "The Rat Pack was a fun group to work with, too, although it was sad to watch the breakup of Sonny and Cher."

It wasn't the GII's only media exposure. The plane made an appearance in the movie Disappearance of Flight 412 starring Glen Ford, and it could be seen taking off each week in the opening segment for the TV show Hart to Hart, a clip of which can be seen at https://youtu.be/ilNUh4L0OhA.

"I felt sorry for the cameraman capturing that scene because our pilot calculated the exact position on the runway where the plane would take off," Cupery explains. "We had to have burned him as we passed overhead. We were that close to him."

The GII held such fond memories for Cupery that when the aircraft's interior was redesigned, he acquired all the seats and kept them in storage for nearly 45 years. He recently acquired a 1972 Econoline van with 72,000 miles

on it, then gutted the interior and rebuilt it using the original chairs and galley from the GII.

"I get a kick out of taking it to car shows because everyone wants to sit in the same chairs Elvis and Sonny and Cher sat in when they were at the peak of their careers," he explains.

CHANGING CAREERS

Although shuttling celebrities was an enjoyable and often envious experience, Cupery opted to give it up when his son, Ryan, was born. He realized he was spending too much time away from his family when Ryan learned to walk while he was on a five-week globetrotting tour.

However, he developed such a strong reputation within Northrop that finding a new job was easy. He went to work for the marketing and public relations department as a spokesman for the F-5 aircraft and served as a liaison for General Electric and Northrop meetings with engineers as the F-17 was being developed. He also conducted tours of the assembly plant and taught classes for engineers on how the jets were manufactured.

Later, he worked as the head of international quality assurance working with companies around the world to build add-on products to Northrop standards. For example, if a country was going to buy a jet, the contract might specify that a specific part, like a wing-tip, be built in that country. It was Cupery's job to ensure

the parts were built to Northrop quality standards.

"I learned a lot about politics in that position. It was an education I'd never be able to buy," he says. "In fact, every job I have held prepared me to start my own business, which succeeded beyond my wildest imagination."

While overseeing quality, Cupery completed a bachelor's business administration degree from the University of Redlands in Redlands, Calif. In one of the courses, a term paper he wrote was actually used to train future students, he notes.

While flying around the world, Cupery developed close friendships with the directors of maintenance at every major airport — relationships that would one day pay huge dividends for him.

"At the time, I wasn't even aware I was developing my future customer list," he explains.

Years earlier, while working as the GII flight engineer, Cupery was tasked with replacing the aircraft windows. The pilot was pretty demanding in how the aircraft looked. Everything needed to be first class, right down to the way the carpet was vacuumed so footprints wouldn't be visible when passengers entered the plane. To maintain a tip-top appearance, the windows had to be replaced every few years.

"But, as the director of maintenance, I had a budget to keep and replacing windows was very

Within a year, he outgrew that facility and bought an industrial property next door. Soon, he had so many windows to repair that he needed to store them in the parking lot. Cupery invested the first $10,000 he made into creating a professional brochure that he mailed to his DOM friends worldwide. When they learned they could repair windows for 75 to 90 percent less than the cost of replacing them, business took off quickly.

"I asked for a leave of absence to grow the company even faster, but Northrop officials said I was too valuable to leave, so I wound up quitting in 1981," Cupery explains. "It was a big risk for me with two small children at home. But, I felt in my heart that I needed to give it a try. Besides, I was confident that if it didn't work out, I could always return to Northrop in some capacity."

Eventually, he acquired another parcel of property to create a 6,000-square-foot repair facility, which is still more than enough space to meet current business demand. But, Cupery wasn't done innovating.

SEEING THE LIGHT

His reputation in the aviation industry for saving money resulted in Marty Owens, with Dassault Falcon Jet, approaching him with a problem. His company had to replace landing light lenses on the Falcon 50 after only 100 hours of use because the material became so opaque that light wouldn't shine through the lens.

Fortunately, Cupery's uncle, Martin Cupery, was a chemist, and he formulated a proprietary coating that was then baked onto the lens. After testing the product for one year, there was no sign of wear on the coating, which meant the lenses didn't need to be replaced.

"Customers were so happy with the coating on the landing lights that they wanted me to do the same thing on navigation lights," he explains. "Today, companies buy lenses and ship them to us where we remove any defects, apply the coating to any polycarbonate material, and ship them back."

Since developing the coating, Cupery had only one lens returned after five years of use. His staff fixed it up and shipped it back to the firm in Germany. He hasn't had any other returns and, today, his company is certified to apply the coating to any lens.

PROUD OF SAFETY RECORD

Of all the things he has accomplished in his career spanning 55 years in the aviation industry, Cupery is most proud of all the money he has saved companies around the world while improving safety at the same time.

"The fact that I could improve safety means a great deal to me," he explains. "In the past, windows would blow out of aircraft all the time because replacing windows was so expensive that people defered maintenance. Today, it is rare to hear reports of a blown-out window. The ability to help make aircraft lights burn brighter is just icing on the cake."

Cupery has so much fun working, he can't imagine retirement, although he does manage to squeeze in more fishing expeditions into his schedule. Plus, he gets to spend more leisure time with his wife, Kathi.

"I could not have laid out my life any better," he added, citing his faith in God for opening his eyes to new opportunities as they emerged. "He laid out my path. I just needed to follow his direction. Rather than just asking for things all the time, I started thanking God for everything he has already done — and God gave me even more than I ever desired." ■

expensive," he explains. "So, after replacing the windows, I asked my boss if I could take the old ones home to see what I could do with them."

Cupery disassembled them, polished up the glass, and resealed the windows. Using an ultrasound machine he bought for $3,000, a lot of money for him back then, he was able to measure the thickness of the windows to 1/10,000th of an inch.

"I showed my boss what I had done and he told me to put them back on the airplane," he added. "That's how Aircraft Window Repairs (www.awrepairs.com) was founded in 1979."

Over the next few years, he developed the FAA's first manual for window repair stations from his tiny warehouse office.

"I knew the FAA would never approve my garage as a repair station, so I rented a small building in an industrial center where I could hang my repair station shingle," he explains. "It had no air conditioning and one old phone that sat on a home-built desk, but the FAA approved the setup."

Robert Cupery

Growing Up With Pontiacs

The Legend 16 June 2014

My GTO was featured in GTO Magazine in June 2014

Meet held by Southern California Gathering of Goats club in 1988. First place went to what I call a "flower pot," a car that is only driven to car shows. Not for me, I think that these beauties must be driven and enjoyed by everyone. Surprisingly, the only part, possibly the most important part of the vehicle that does not work, is the radio.

The car wasn't considered as nice then as it is now! Even Mr. GTO himself (Mr. Jim Wangers) checked it out and commented "Great Car," a very nice compliment.

The engine I removed for overhaul had four cracked pistons, needed a new cam, and bored out .030 over. There was no rushing on doing this, as the engine compartment really needed a good cleaning. The transmission needed to be rebuilt as well as the rear end. The top had seen better days so a new one was installed over the freshly painted frame.

I removed the dash and installed a new wiring harness and took the instruments apart for cleaning. What appeared to be rust on them was nothing more than actually dried out foam rubber padding thus everything cleaned up beautifully.

The metal fan shroud I located in Michigan (aftermarket ones are plastic) the top latch was the hardest to find but I got lucky and found one in *Hemmings*. The local GTO club, Southern California Gathering of Goats, was very helpful and encouraged me to continue working on the car. Thanks for Barry Troup, Carter Chee, Dave Anderson, and the genius Heinrich Gerhardt just to name a few.

That was already thirty years ago and so here is my son "Ryan" pictured next to the car, proudly holding the second place trophy for Western Regional

Both my children, Jennifer and Ryan learned how to drive a stick shift in this car. Ryan spent many hours cleaning and touching it up. My wife Kathi and our daughter enjoyed most of the cruising and getting the thumbs up.

In 1990, my own company, founded in 1979, "Aircraft Window Repairs," set out to establish an East Coast facility to go along side the West Coast sector. So we loaded up the goat with our newer addition at the time, which was the 1966 Mustang GT.

After numerous shows and fun in Florida, we decided to move back to California in 2000, loading up the cars for yet another trip. I was happy to see them returned to me safely after the

transporting driver had endured a flat tire and while on the side of the highway had groups of people either stopping or turning around to ask if the GTO was available for sale! This was something that the driver had never experienced before.

Since our return to California, the Mustang had been sold but my loyalty stayed strong alongside the GTO. I was very honored to be asked by David Newhart if he could photograph our GTO for the tabletop book titled *Pontiac's Great One – GTO* written in 2009 by Darwin Holmstrom. It is pictured six

times in Chapter Two on pages 53, 80, 82, 83 and 84. My pay in return was to receive an autographed book from Mr. Newhart himself -- and I am still expecting it any day now, I hope.

So in closing, I got my new car, my family has had fun with it and I sure do miss the Pontiac line. I almost had the car in the Barrett-Jackson auction last year but when I asked where do I put the reserve, they advised me there wasn't a reserve, so I pulled it off the block. Just couldn't see someone steal it from me after all of the hard work and TLC that had been put into it. Best regards to all my GTO friends.

Chapter 16

Postcards to my parents

Whenever I was traveling, I would try to send some postcards to my parents to convey the type of whirlwind trips I was making. However, regardless of where I was in the world, I always managed to communicate with my folks back home in Wisconsin. Here are some samples of the cards I sent to my parents.

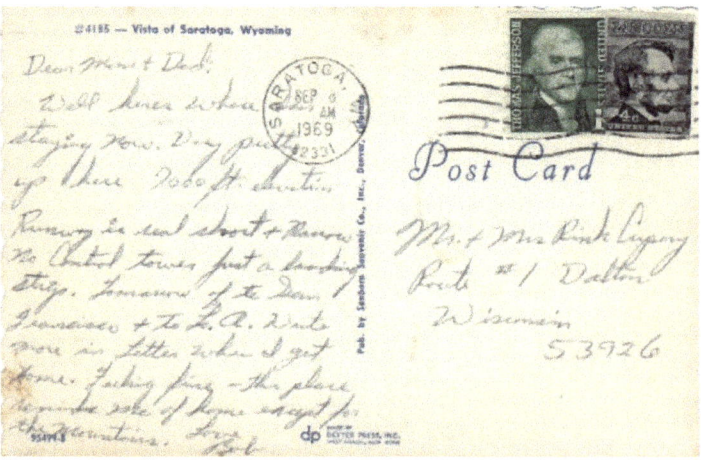

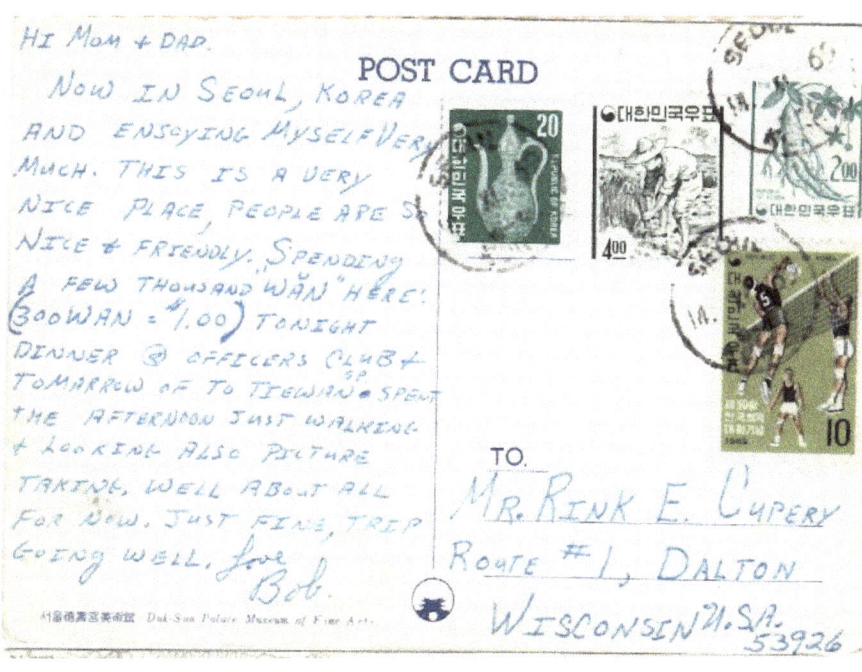

HI MOM + DAD.

NOW IN SEOUL, KOREA
AND ENJOYING MYSELF VERY
MUCH. THIS IS A VERY
NICE PLACE, PEOPLE ARE SO
NICE + FRIENDLY. SPENDING
A FEW THOUSAND "WAN" HERE!
(300 WAN = $1.00) TONIGHT
DINNER @ OFFICERS CLUB +
TOMORROW OF TO TIEWAN SPENT
THE AFTERNOON JUST WALKING
+ LOOKING ALSO PICTURE
TAKING, WELL ABOUT ALL
FOR NOW. JUST FINE, TRIP
GOING WELL. love
Bob.

TO.
MR. RINK E. CUPERY
ROUTE #1, DALTON
WISCONSIN U.S.A.
53926

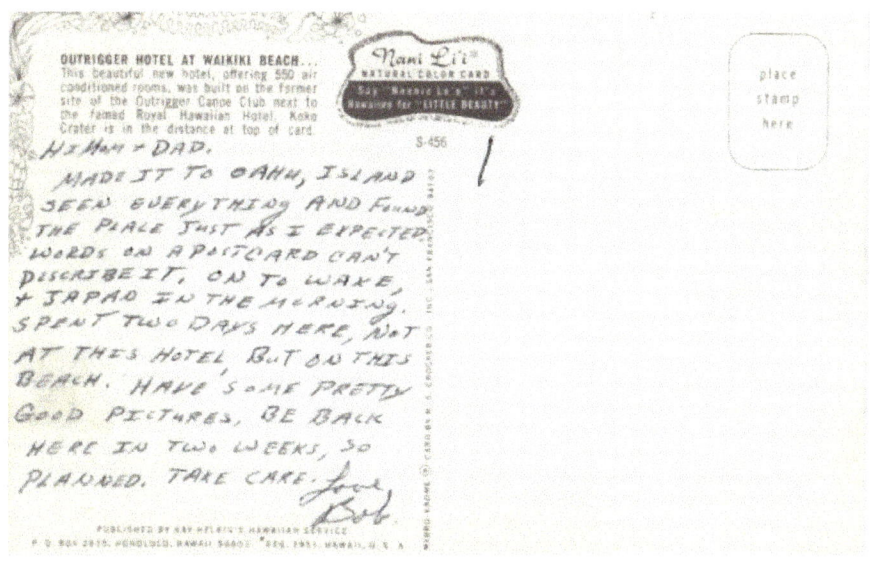

HI MOM + DAD.
MADE IT TO OAHU, ISLAND
SEEN EVERYTHING AND FOUND
THE PLACE JUST AS I EXPECTED
WORDS ON A POSTCARD CAN'T
DESCRIBE IT, ON TO WAKE,
+ JAPAN IN THE MORNING.
SPENT TWO DAYS HERE, NOT
AT THIS HOTEL, BUT ON THIS
BEACH. HAVE SOME PRETTY
GOOD PICTURES, BE BACK
HERE IN TWO WEEKS, SO
PLANNED. TAKE CARE. love
Bob.

MOATS AND WALLS OF FORT PULASKI, Savannah, Ga.
This fort, constructed 1829-46 for defense of the Savannah River, is a fine example of 19th Century military architecture. A National Park Service Area.

Hi Mom & DAD (you ALL)

WELL I'm STILL KICKING
AROUND THE SOUTH. HOPE ALL IS
OKAY FROM OPERATION. Suppose
YOUR SICK OF SITTING AROUND.
THE SOUTHERN BELLS ARE REAL
GOOD TO ME. HA-HA

I VISITED THIS FORT, SURE
GIVES YOU AN IDEA OF 1st HOW US.
PROTECTED AGAINST FOREIGN AGRESS.
THEN OF WHAT IT MENT IN THE
CIVEL WAR. IT PERFECT WEATHER
& I FEEL PERFECT TOO. I FINALLY
GOT USE TO TIME CHANGE. WRITE
LATER ON. BYE Now Love

Ektachrome by Walter H. Miller
63171

Bob

Save PLACE STAMP HERE

Bob

POST CARD

MR. & MRS. RINK E. Cupery
ROUTE #1 DALTON
WISCONSIN (53926)

George Washington devoted much of his time during the years 1783-1789 to the development of the Bowling Green and adjacent areas, a part of which is seen in this view of the Mansion West Front.

Hi Mom & DAD. —

JUST TO LET YOU KNOW
THAT GOT BACK TO L.A.
OKAY & NOW IN WASH.
LEAVING TO DAY FOR
NEW YORK. WAS REAL
NICE TO SEE YOU A
FEW HRS IN CHICAGO LAST
WEEK. MUST RUN NOW
Love Bob.

Distributed by L. B. Prince Co., Fairfax, Va.   PE 103

AMERICAN LEGION
50TH ANNIVERSARY
1919 – 1969

ADDRESS

Mr. & Mrs. Rink Cupery
Route #1
DALTON
WISCONSIN
53926